Finding Flamenco

Finding Flamenco

STEPHANY BORGES

ARCHWAY
PUBLISHING

Archway Publishing books may be ordered
through booksellers or by contacting:

Archway Publishing
1663 Liberty Drive
Bloomington, IN 47403
www.archwaypublishing.com
1 (888) 242-5904

All Drawings By: Ronald Joseph Chavez

ISBN: 978-1-4808-8396-3 (sc)
ISBN: 978-1-4808-8395-6 (e)

Library of Congress Control Number: 2019915928

Print information available on the last page.

Archway Publishing rev. date: 11/5/2019

"To all my teachers, especially my children"

duende : inspiration or passion, especially flamenco

Contents

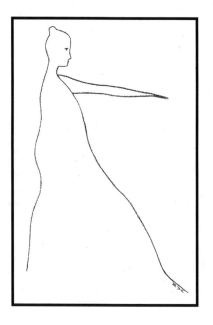

Chapter One
The Leap

So then, the *duende* is a force not a
labor, a struggle not a thought.
—Garcia Lorca, "Theory and Play of the Duende"

I am getting to that age, sixty and beyond, approaching
new limits and hard-won freedoms. In astrological circles this transition is called a Saturn return. This cycle of
Saturn every twenty-nine years reflects the natural pro-
gression of a life, the movement from youth to maturity,
from maturity to wisdom, and for some who live into their
late eighties, from wisdom to spirit. Each transition has its
own challenges and requirements. Whether I am experiencing a Saturn return or a natural life cycle, one thing is
for sure: it's a real blizzard in my psyche and outside my
window. After all the energy I've used trying to find my
way, here is where I am. It's a cold winter's day in New
Mexico. Snow falls.

I've gone and done it—retired from teaching at a university in California, sold my house in Northern California,
and moved to New Mexico. Though much rehearsed and
carefully orchestrated, the reality of leaving my job, my
community, and my home in the redwoods to live a new
life in the high desert has not been easy. In many ways it

has been extraordinarily difficult. If I could turn back the clock, perhaps I wouldn't do it at all. If not for a series of fateful events, such as selling my house in a day for a listing price I thought no one would pay, I might still be living and working in California. Shortly after my move, the real estate market fell apart along with the broader economy. I would have been, with the majority of workers in the United States, afraid to retire before sixty or even at all.

No one likes for me to talk about being old any more than about death and dying. I'm not morbid, but to me, sixty is old—old enough for me to be free to do some of the things I want to do without regret, fear, or anxiety. My mother died when she was sixty-seven, my father died at thirty-five, and none of my grandparents lived to see seventy. People talk about sixty being the new forty. They might be right, but I am hedging my bets. Maybe this is why I think it's now or never. I am curious about how I will fill this gap, this gift of open time. Teaching English and creative writing supported me financially over the years. As a writer, I don't think of retirement the way some people do. My day job was always a means to an end, even when it consumed me utterly.

I expect I'll write because I always do. Perhaps I will take art classes and deepen my yoga practice. The unplanned life excites me. Yet finding flamenco surprised me. It never occurred to me that my abiding love of dance would be resurrected at this stage in my life. My attraction to flamenco awakened over fifty years ago at the Old Spaghetti Factory Café and Excelsior Coffee House in San Francisco. When I mention the Old Spaghetti Factory, people think of a popular chain of restaurants. "No," I say. "Not that one. The Old Spaghetti Factory on Grant and Green is gone." Just like locals called San Francisco "the City," we also called the Old Spaghetti Factory Café and Excelsior Coffee House simply the Old Spaghetti Factory.

The Old Spaghetti Factory was one of a kind, a bohemian hangout run by the infamous, much-loved patron of the arts Frederick H. Kuh. His friends called him Freddie. He hired actors, painters, poets, and dancers to wait tables, cook, and tend bar so that they could support themselves while doing their art. North Beach attracted artists like a warm sun in a cooling solar system. Some of the artists made it big, like Allen Ginsberg, the Beat poet, and Kaffe Faucett, the fiber artist. Most died poor and unknown, like Ronnie, my favorite waiter. No matter, they shared passion for all that is spontaneous, organic, and creative.

Many people sought refuge in Freddie's restaurant. In the fifties and sixties, even in San Francisco, people were seldom "out of the closet" except in closed social circles. In addition to being a patron of the arts, Freddie created a safe haven for a generation of remarkable homosexual men who were devoted to him and to the establishment. Freddie had a knack for business and for creating community, with family money to back him. He called himself a bohemian entrepreneur and became as successful in his own right as his Chicago stockbroker father had been in his.

My mother waited tables on the weekends while she went to college to become a teacher. Though she was an x-ray technician, she had yearned to go to college all her life. She was a single parent with two girls, far from her immigrant roots in Chicago, and those years working and going to school were some of the best in her life. She would bring me and my little sister with her to work, and the cooks would serve us dishes of spaghetti with meat sauce in the kitchen at the big round table. The cooks stood behind a long aluminum counter, stirring huge steaming pots on two industrial stoves. They wore tall white hats and matching aprons and seldom smiled, intent on their tasks. The waiters would hurry back and forth in a variety of moods, depending on their customers. I delighted in the fragrant warmth of that kitchen. The hustle and bustle and hum of the collective effort unfolded like a choreographed performance as another Friday or Saturday night took off.

As the sun went down, I would walk my little sister several blocks back to Fisherman's Wharf and the housing projects where we lived. We spent the evenings watching our small nine-inch television perched aloft an upended packing crate with Chinese characters down one side. We used TV tables as little desks and drew endless pictures on the orange paper from the boxes of x-ray film from our mother's work. Essentially a latchkey kid, I experienced our lives as very bohemian and rich with promise. I disliked the projects because they were ugly and the kids were mean, but living in North Beach seemed to be as good as living on the Left Bank in Paris, where Freddie lived half the year.

At no more than thirty, Freddie looked like a blond, blue-eyed cherub with golden curls. He wore a blue and white Turkish bead on a leather cord around his neck to ward off the evil eye. Each year in Paris, he hung out with poets and painters. Everyone soldiered on in his absence, and his return was always a cause for celebration. An independently wealthy connoisseur and serious collector of all things Victorian, he haunted estate sales and auctions. He lived on the top floor of the restaurant in a four-thousand-square-foot loft with narrow aisles between his antique lamps, dressers, tables, cabinets, and statues. In his own retirement he would sell the Old Spaghetti Factory and another restaurant he had opened a few blocks away, the Savoy Tivoli, and would live another fifteen years on his estate in St. Helena named Le Vieux Reve, as if he had just stepped out of a Jane Austen novel. He died suddenly of a cerebral hemorrhage at seventy, a portly, contented, landed gentleman of the arts.

I had an enormous crush on Freddie. When I learned that women were out of the question for him, in my dreamy, adolescent way I hoped that somehow he would make an exception for me. I imagined myself his life companion. I would happily live with him in his self-created, opulent world. I would sit with him on his hand-carved, brocade- and velvet-covered couches and sleep beside him in his huge four-poster bed piled with feather mattresses and silk pillows. I would travel to France and dine with him in fine restaurants. It would be like living in a Henry James novel. Looking back, I am sure everyone had a crush on Freddie, my mother included. Part of his great appeal was his iconic loneliness. It made him just out of reach and sensationally irresistible.

He rented out a back room of what had actually once been a real spaghetti factory in the 1930s and '40s to his friend Richard Waylen, a sculptor. Dick, as he was called, managed the flamenco troupe that danced there on week-ends. A thin and severe-looking man, he dressed in dra-matic black capes and hats. When I came to the shows, first alone and then with my "hippie" friends, his angular face registered a resigned displeasure. Barely fourteen, I knew from the first note of the flamenco guitar and the first throaty cry of the singer that I had found a world of music and dance that thrilled me to the core. I had another huge crush on the thin, blond singer called Rubio. His melan-choly introversion and his long white hands that he crossed over his chest as he sang drew me into his soulful laments. My open adoration must have been incredibly annoying or incredibly flattering. One thing was for sure—it showed.

I was studying modern dance and ballet, but neither of these dance forms had the immediacy and the passion of flamenco. The small stage and the intimacy of the room, with its low wooden benches, encouraged a vital connec-tion between the dancers and audience. The Flamenco de la Bodega was a true, small-scale cabaret, perhaps San Francisco's first. Flamenco had an intensity and a raw beauty I had never experienced before. Maybe I had, but only in passing, as I watched a sunset over the San Francisco Bay or stood in a grove of redwoods while the sun filtered through the tall limbs overhead. Instantly, I was hooked. Young, dewy-eyed, and impressionable, I was tolerated in this unusual world of adults. Occasionally, I watched the early-evening show before being given the boot.

My years growing up in the City, especially in North Beach, exposed me to the arts and to the Beat way of life. I embraced the romantic notion that people were more than their jobs or possessions. Too poor to idealize being a starving artist, I did well in school. I planned on becoming a doctor or some sort of researcher who would help discover cures for life-threatening diseases. No matter how illustrious my imagined career, I also envisioned a time when sufficient funds would allow me to live a spontaneous, creative life. So when I left my university job decades later, I was doing more than retiring: I was embarking on an adventure in living, abounding with freedom and possibility.

My academic work on D. H. Lawrence brought me to Taos, New Mexico, several times, for conferences and for research. I am sure you have heard stories about Easterners like Georgia O'Keefe driving to the West Coast, stopping in Santa Fe, having an epiphany or something like it, and deciding to stay (or come back as soon as possible). I remember the first time we stopped at La Fonda in Santa Fe for lunch. I sat in the patio-like enclosed courtyard surrounded by hand-painted glass windowpanes and wept. I reassured my concerned family, "I am so happy, just so happy." I hadn't known such a place existed. The light, the hushed sound within the round adobe walls, and the ineffable sense of presence drew me back year after year. New Mexico is called the Land of Enchantment for a reason.

The image of the phoenix that D. H. Lawrence held dear beckoned me as my retirement approached. What a perfect symbol for dynamic change. This bird, as legendary as the dragon, rises up from the ashes of its former life to live with renewed vigor. Whenever I visited Taos, I always tried to get up to the Lawrence Ranch, as it is called. The short walk from the main house to the small shrine housing his ashes became a personal pilgrimage over the years. On my first visit as a resident and not a visitor, I opened myself up to inspiration. I gave thanks for the opportunity to return to this whimsical chapel overlooking the Taos Gorge and the wide-open Taos Valley. A plaster phoenix over the entrance and another above the altar within reminded me to welcome transformation, no matter how difficult. Yet when I had dreamed of New Mexico, I had dreamed of Taos, never Albuquerque.

Albuquerque was a city I had flown in and out of on my way to Santa Fe and Taos. Over the years, though, my life had changed, and after my remarriage, my husband and I found a compromise as we neared our respective retirements. He wanted to leave his law practice and go to graduate school and read and think about history, and I wanted to write in New Mexico. After living a more rural existence in Northern California, I welcomed a larger city with more culture and services. Albuquerque met our needs, a genial compromise.

It had never occurred to me that Albuquerque was the hub of the flamenco world in the United States. Seeing advertisements for the Flamenco Festival that first unbearably hot, dry summer, I reminisced about my old passion and considered taking classes at the conservatory. One more possibility on the list of things to explore. It took many months before I did, expecting it to be a quick tribute to something long past. I walked into my introductory class with no idea that I had stepped into the next chapter of my life. How was it possible that something I had responded to completely as a teenager had the same capacity to captivate me now?

On that first evening, I found myself in a hot, cramped studio. Facing a bank of dusty mirrors, I danced with girls and boys and men and women who were trying their hardest to follow the rhythmic footwork our teacher demonstrated. Our teacher, a tall, thin, and rather irritable young woman, demanded absolute attention. I left that first half-hour class exhilarated, memory traces of old songs and dances flowing inside of me. When I stepped outside, the New Mexican sunset blazed overhead. I had magically rediscovered the ambience of the Old Spaghetti Factory, with its vivid cast of characters, fifty years later and in a city far from San Francisco.

Driving home, I listened to Bob Marley sing, "Everything's gonna be alright, the gun man's in the house tonight, but everything's gonna be all right." On Route 66, I passed the now-familiar pawnshops selling guns and turquoise, Mexican restaurants known for their smoky red and green chili, and cheap hotels sheltering the poor and aimless. To the east, the Sandia Mountains turned purple as the electric-blue sky sucked the light from the land. To the west, the clear lines of the volcanic mesa glowed liked embers on the edge of the world.

The flamenco studio has the same handmade, creative atmosphere of the Old Spaghetti Factory, a world apart from the ordinary world. In this space, we swim like fish in the healing waters of music and song, a school of inexperienced dancers, frolicking in the warm currents. I love flamenco. I love our studio. When I open the door, the clean, musty smell of warm bodies, the ratta-tatta-tat of footwork on the battered wooden floors, the plaintive sounds of the guitar, and the syncopated rhythms of hand clapping, called *palmas*, go straight to my heart. I am doing what I came all the way from California to do. And this time I am not fourteen. I alternate between feeling as if I am a foolish old woman who has fallen in love with a man far too young and feeling like a woman who has just caught the last bus out of Tijuana in the middle of the night. The overarching sensations are sheer gratitude and relief. I have arrived just in the nick of time.

Chapter Two
A Dash of Obsession

To get the creative habit, you need a working
environment that's habit forming.
—Twyla Tharp (choreographer/dancer), *The Creative Habit*

A story circulates about Carmen Amaya, the Gypsy
who revolutionized flamenco dance for women. She
wore pants and emphasized her footwork, refusing to be
confined to long, heavy skirts or limited only to hip and
arm movements. The story goes that she had been born
with kidneys that failed to develop and that remained the
size of a child's. Dancing at peak intensity, sweating out the
toxins in her blood, she was literally saving her own life.
Though she eventually died of kidney failure in her fifties,
she might have died much sooner had she not danced. I feel
a deep kinship with Carmen Amaya. Dancing keeps my
spirit alive and my life from feeling like a worn-out habit.

Last night I entered the studio for the first time since
the Christmas break. Seeing the other dancers straggle
in from the dark, cold, icy streets and into a new year, I
rejoiced. I could tell they felt the same way I did about
coming back to this life on the other side of the weather,
the holidays, and the winter colds. We had made it back.
We were together again. It was a miracle of sorts. This is

not about friendship. Except for one or two, I don't see any of these people anywhere else. Our shared passion for this creative process unites us in an experience that is nonverbal, immediate, and transcending of age. At any given time, the dancers in the studio range from three to over seventy.

Few places impart such a mysterious influence. I don't feel it in the convenient and modern house I live in or in the yoga studio I go to with its bamboo floors and pictures of the Dalai Lama. I felt it in the sixties when I danced at the Avalon Ballroom in San Francisco to the tunes of the Grateful Dead and Big Brother and the Holding Company. This was before anyone became famous or died, a time of potent and largely uncharted beginnings. Janis Joplin had just arrived from a place in Texas no one had ever heard of except Chet Helms. A young entrepreneur from Texas, Chet had opened a space called the Avalon Ballroom, the first sixties rock-and-roll venue. Long, straight, blond hair framed his long, pale face. His electric blue eyes were magnified by round, gold wire–rimmed glasses. He invited everyone into his large flat in the bottom of a two-story Victorian building in the Haight. Certain times in my life and certain people I have encountered have left behind traces of this kind of magic.

The seductive power of the studio draws us in night after night, month after month. Located in a run-down section of downtown Albuquerque, two blocks north of the Rescue Mission and two blocks west of the train station, our old building runs long on a narrow lot. A warren of four studios—two large, front and back, and two small in the center—the conservatory evokes the bohemian atmosphere of a Greenwich Village loft. I find myself craving its sound, its light, and its warmth. I don't have to force myself to arrive on time, to be fully present.

High ceilings with crown molding and white plaster walls autographed by passing artists give the studio a unique ambience. The wood floors are battered to a chalky patina from the pounding of flamenco boots and shoes. It's a tight, raw, labyrinthine space of dark and light, a portal into a world of ancient melodies, rhythms, and song. We leave behind the ordinary world of work and home and duty and enter what I experience as a mythic place.

I can be beautiful, sad, rich, poor, elegant, and loud. I can be too much or too little and sometimes just right. When class begins and the teacher puts on an extravagant, slow *seguidilla,* the singer's plaintive voice cuts to the bone. We bend forward, letting our arms dangle, our necks lengthen, our heads release toward the floor. So begins our sequence of stretches, warming up our bodies. We enter a sacred space where music and movement silence the mind and awaken the heart. Fluid memories barely out of reach of consciousness spontaneously arise. As we move into our standing poses, arms lifted overhead, I experience a calm vitality. Dance is and has been a way of opening to the moment, to the truth of the experience of the infinite in a finite body. Kinetic form metabolizes daily concerns: worries, doubts, and thoughts themselves vitalize me. Everything becomes fuel for movement as my senses experience a dimension that brings increased awareness. I knock at the door to the universe and, more often than not, am given permission to enter.

Our studio reminds me of the Trieste Café in North Beach, San Francisco. Signed photographs of movie stars and Italian opera singers decorate the faded yellow walls. Distinctive signatures document sixty years of the café's existence. Such an atmosphere can't be bought or decorated into existence. These places have soul, in the real sense of the word, providing environments for creative process to begin again and again.

A few years ago, I went back to the Trieste after a longer absence than usual. The staff, many of them relatives of the original owner, had grown old. One of my favorite people, a woman who had served me wonderful cappuccinos since I was a rebellious teenager and who always recognized me in my many incarnations, was happy to see me but clearly had been ill. She had lost a lot of weight and her usual rosy complexion, but her henna-dyed hair burned as bright orange as ever. When I inquired about her health, she said she had been battling cancer for a while. As I sat at a round mosaic table that had been in the same spot for years, melancholy pierced my heart. The touchstones in my life were passing, age and time erasing the familiar faces that were North Beach to me.

Someone put an Italian opera on the jukebox, and suddenly, the woman and the young man working with her behind the counter stepped into the room and sang, their strong, clear voices flooding the café with emotion. Everyone stopped talking and listened, many with tears in their eyes, united in this shared, unrepeatable moment of beauty. Wonder and awe filled the café in the presence of *el duende*, that insatiable passion of the moment. When the song ended, the singers returned to making and serving coffee, to routines they had observed for decades. Things might have looked the same, but we, the patrons, had been transformed.

I took my daughter to Lisbon when she turned twenty-one. We went to a fado bar in the old town. Fado has some of the characteristics of flamenco. A true fado singer can turn an audience's heart inside out, the way Carmen Amaya could do when she danced. The singer's success is measured in tears. The audience comes to cry. *Duende* cannot be reproduced. It must be experienced for oneself, and the artist can't fake it either. Everyone knows whether it was present or not. There is no explaining it and no questioning it. In a sense, it is completely irrational, completely natural, and completely unique every time.

The flamenco studio reminds me of that fado bar in Lisbon and the Trieste Café in San Francisco. As class begins, my breath deepens, and my pulse quickens. All of us are in the unrepeatable moment, in our bodies, in our hearts, and in our minds. Life becomes fresh and alive, exciting and beautiful. The Navajos have a word for it: *hozo.* I dance for the times that are close to an epiphany but closer to the experience of *duende.* Epiphany is too abstract. *Duende* lives in the blood, in the spirit, at the root of things. Sorrow, love, betrayal, hate, and loss all have a place to coexist. The opposites that normally pull the beauty of desire asunder are mystically united.

A creative habit has a dash of obsession to it. Addiction can be a hindrance and a blessing. Being addicted to an art form is a new experience for me. I savor being a beginner with no professional goals. Of course, I want to learn and be a better dancer, but I dance for the pleasure of the immediate experience. I have learned a valuable lesson. To do anything well, I must fall in love, deeply and completely, with the process.

I petition the powers that be, *Please let this unexpected joy last long enough to take me to a place where I can really dance without counting out the steps and breaking sequences into little units I haltingly string together.* Then, if I am fortunate, a new level of craft might begin. My unfolding relationship to the rhythms, songs, and patterns that have lived through centuries have brought color, drama, and passion to my life just when I thought it was fading. I am learning a new language, tapped out in intricate codes. I am learning my way into a world that maps the stories of trees and leaves, the spaces between birth and death, in music and dance.

It is said that people who watched Carmen Amaya dance often wept. She could just walk onto a stage, and even people who had never seen her before burst into tears. People who go to hear fado singers go with the intention of crying. This kind of crying is cathartic, a release of pent-up emotions. We need to cry together as much as we need to laugh together. Carmen Amaya radiated a unique power and energy that was instantaneous. What is this power? Where does it come from? *Duende* taps the source of creation, the light and the dark, the good and the bad, embracing all the conflicting emotions and desires of a lifetime into a single moment in time.

Chapter Three
When I Grow Up

More important to culture than social
fabric is the necessity of imagination.
—James Hillman, *The Soul's Code*

A photograph holds one of my earliest memories. I must be three. I'm in a little rocking chair. I feel content though I am all by myself. Probably my mother was in the other room writing letters at the kitchen table or making supper. It was just the two of us at that point since my father died. I had been playing dress-up all afternoon. My grandmother and her eight sisters were seamstresses and delighted in giving me their old finery, as they called it. The steamer trunk my Austrian grandmother brought with her from Vienna overflowed with sequined shawls, lacy fans, and long strings of sparkling beads. There were slips and scarves, gloves and hats. Feathers sagged from lovely felt brims. I had a mirror on the inside of the closet door. When I played dress-up, my mother opened the door for me so I could see how my costumes looked. When I looked in the mirror, I was always delighted.

Pretty things enrapture me. I trace this characteristic to those early moments of play surrounded by shine and glitter, the soft feel of real silk, the snowflake patterns in handmade lace. In the photo, a hand-embroidered shawl with fringe as long as my arms is wrapped tightly around my body like a big gorgeous blanket. I recall rocking and singing, "Row, row, row your boat" at the top of my lungs. I sang it over and over in glee. "Merrily, merrily, merrily, merrily … life is but a dream."

In another photographed memory, I sit on the back porch in a handmade cotton slip. It is summer, and I am barefoot. My feet are perfect and strong, and my body is healthy and plump. My face is framed by a tangle of curls. I might have passed for Shirley Temple. What draws me to this memory is the expression I have of being so satisfied with life. It is enough to be the girl in the pretty white slip, her chubby feet planted on the warm wooden steps on a sunny day.

Another memory is not a photograph. It was the first week of kindergarten. Our teacher was asking us questions to get us to talk in a group. She sat on a chair while we sat on the floor in a circle around her. The teacher asked each of us, "What do you want to be when you grow up?"

We were arranged alphabetically, and I suppose because my last name starts with a B, I was called upon to speak first. Or maybe I volunteered, ever ready to excel. Without hesitation, I said, "A peacock."

The teacher's eyes widened with surprise. The other children looked at her, wondering if people could indeed grow up to become peacocks. We were only five years old and not quite sure what it meant to grow up after all.

The teacher shook her head and laughed. I felt better then. But she clearly wanted something more from me.

"You can't grow up and become a peacock. You can become a teacher or a wife and mother."

I was embarrassed now. I quickly responded, "A teacher." I was rewarded with a nod and a smile as she moved on to a boy who replied, "A fireman."

Now almost sixty years later, I sit in a tiny room in the back of the main studio on a box called a *cajon*. A percussion instrument, it is the only piece of furniture in the room. I need a place to sit while I put on my handmade, red suede flamenco shoes. Dressed in a navy blue shirt with small white polka dots and a double ruffle along the bottom, I glance up while tying my shoelaces and see myself in the mirror. The woman and the little girl meet in this moment. I recognize her in the joy I see in my eyes. I straighten and smooth my hair. I feel affection for the child who could imagine growing up and becoming a peacock! In finding flamenco, I find lost selves scattered through time, like autumn leaves beneath a tree. Finally, as a woman, I can dress up and stamp my feet in the name of truth and beauty.

My mother grew up a child of immigrant parents in Chicago. Both of her parents, her father from Copenhagen and her mother from Vienna, arrived in the United States in their late twenties with solid trades and ambitions. Initially, their dry-cleaning business thrived, but during the Great Depression and its aftermath, they lost everything they had built and bought. They lost their businesses, their country house, and their new car. Bright, curious, and ambitious, my mother yearned to move upward in American society and away from her "ethnic" roots and her increasingly alcoholic father. She eradicated all the German words from her mind and traces of the accent from her speech, though she and her mother spoke only in German until her mother died.

Her mother's long illness and death interrupted my mother's plans to go to the University of Chicago and study journalism. Instead, after her mother's death, she became an x-ray technician and joined the army as an officer in a medical unit at Fort Ord, California. No matter what, her daughters would be college-educated. We would have the opportunity to satisfy our intellectual curiosity and enter the ranks of the professional classes. She secretly hoped a day would arrive when she could go back to college herself.

Though we were poor as a single-parent family, my mother had high standards. We lived with books, music, good food, and art. We were expected to do well in school. In junior high I took dance classes at the community center in North Beach with Gloria Unti, an Italian woman with a long braid down her back. She wore no makeup and preferred loose-fitting cotton clothes and her signature rubber zoris in a time when women wore nylons and high heels and styled their hair. Gloria taught the Martha Graham technique and encouraged us to live in our bodies in a natural, expressive way. My love affair with dance began. I studied ballet in high school and decided on a Russian ballet school that had the aura of "old world" romance I seemed to crave. I continued to get straight A's to please my mother.

Finally, my mother had to put a stop to it. It was one thing for her daughter to dance after school at the local community center and another for her to become a professional dancer. Nothing but a solid and rigorous college education would do. She said dancers were "all washed up" before they turned forty and "never earned a dime." My mother had strong opinions about a number of things! When I started flamenco lessons as a teenager, I paid for them with my salary from working in my godmother's clothing store, Nasimo's, down the street from the Old Spaghetti Factory. My mother declared that flamenco was an "ethnic" dance that attracted uneducated gypsies. Working her hardest to assimilate and distance herself from the confining German community she had fled in Chicago, my mother had no interest in what we now celebrate as multiculturalism. My desire to become a flamenco dancer met with complete opposition.

I would lie in bed at night and see kinetic shapes moving across the screen in my mind. I realize now that I was choreographing dances as I fell asleep. I gradually gave up on becoming a professional dancer, but I managed to squeeze in dance as a minor while I majored in English literature. What a perfect life that was! After a lecture on Victorian literature, I ran to the dance studio for a modern dance class. I didn't realize how much I needed to maintain a balance between my body and my mind, but I intuitively cobbled together a course of study that did just that. But dance was a hobby, a passion that work and family gradually eclipsed.

James Hillman, a Jungian analyst, believes that a person's calling is a natural inclination that often gets overlooked or completely repressed. This calling has less to do with what the child is forced to do in school than with what the child likes to do in her free time. Play can reveal true inclination. What does the child want to do? Like to do? I had an aptitude for math and science. I enjoyed school and studying. But nothing gave me pleasure equal to dance. Maybe I was good at too many things and afraid to challenge my mother. Whatever the reason, it took finding my way back to flamenco in this last third of life to reconnect to my earliest inclinations.

At a student assembly when she was about six or seven, my daughter proudly announced that she wanted to become an airline stewardess or a waitress. The other young girls who stood at the microphone to announce their intentions to become brain surgeons and astronauts met with approving looks and smiles. My daughter's ambition, so happily proclaimed, seemed to stun the parents around me. On the way home I asked her about her ambitions. She had never seemed interested in making or serving food. She replied, "When I walk around, everyone will look up at me." Then I knew she was speaking her soul's code, reaching for an image that would someday transform her into the head of a company, an actress, or any number of things that would give her the feeling of standing out and being seen.

The image of the peacock was my five-year-old self's way of expressing my love of display and of beauty. Already, in kindergarten, we were being tracked into pre-established paths appropriate for our gender and our class. Rediscovering a world of color, fabrics, bangles, golden earrings, and charms, I have found the treasure of my imagination. I have joined a community of people of all ages and backgrounds, strong people, proud people, yearning people who have generous spirits and emotions.

The little girl in me who loved to sing at the top of her voice has found adult expression. A woman's wisdom combines with a child's irrepressible imagination. I can be tough and feminine without being shamed. For brief moments I can even be fire.

Chapter Four
Sexy but Free

The compulsion to find a lover and husband
in a single person has doomed more women
to misery than any other illusion.
—Carolyn Heilbrun, *Writing a Woman's Life*

The new semester begins. The refinished floors shine.
My shoes stick or slip as I move across the floor or turn.
I preferred the worn smoothness of the old floors, though
they looked shabby and dusty. The room is packed. Soon
our numbers will drop off. But maybe not this year. More
and more people have discovered flamenco. The University
of New Mexico offers a dance degree with a flamenco em-
phasis. Many students from the university come over and
dance at our studio at night. I tend to discover things just
a little ahead of everyone else. I was a flower child before
there was the label. Usually when a person, place, or thing
becomes popular, I am about to walk out the back door. I
hope I don't do that this time because I have found something right for me.

In my introductory class, fifteen of us struggled together, sharing the excitement and the stress of learning
something new, challenging, and dynamic. Now only five
of us are left, bonded not by age or profession but by our

shared desire to learn the next sequence of a dance, to perfect our evolving technique. Another group of enthusiastic novices fills the tiny studio space reserved for the introductory classes. I watch them bond and wonder how many of them will find their way to the next class, *Baile* I, the beginning of the real thing.

In *Baile* I, we study basic technique and traditional dance choreography. We must attend at least two one-hour classes per week. Our teacher's patience for beginners creates a perfect environment for dedication and hard work on the long, arduous road to becoming a flamenco dancer. We know how fortunate we are to be studying with one of the best flamenco teachers, dancers, and choreographers in the country. He never seems to tire of demonstrating steps, singing out the rhythms, or pacing us through endless sequences and repetitions as we learn a dance. When he sings to us, we are transported, as if under a spell. I am thankful that I am not in my twenties, my thirties, or even my forties. I would be trapped inside the cage of my crush.

I taught for a few years at an all-girls Catholic high school. Studies suggest that girls do better in math and science when in a same-sex learning environment. Girls play hard and work hard to excel without the distraction of boys in high school. Emotions and behaviors that would be brought about by having boys in the same room don't get in the way of their focus and concentration. The same studies show that the presence of girls has the opposite effect on boys' achievement. They spar and excel in their quest to impress the girls. Once a month the girls could bring a male friend or boyfriend to campus. The results confirmed the research. These same confident, outspoken young women became hesitant and submissive in the presence of a single young man.

I have begun to savor the mysterious link between eros and creativity. The attraction I often feel for an artist or a holy man draws me to the center of the dance. The yearning is impersonal, immediate, and inspiring. The energy of attraction feeds my craft. Without it, I would certainly find reasons to talk myself out of studying flamenco at all. I know better than to mess up my relationship with myself as a dancer or with my teacher as my mentor. What a gift! The erotic undercurrents in the room invigorate my spirit. I am sure our teacher experiences our adoration, and it energizes him to soldier on with his beginners.

When I taught Introduction to Women's Studies at the university, I included a section on women and creativity. I encouraged students to think about the nature of the "muse" in artists' lives. This inevitably led to considerations of gender. Often, women artists, attracted to the power and the talent of a male artist like Picasso, ended up having babies and insane bouts of jealousy instead of developing their own bodies of work. Just as often, the artist left them for the next muse who lavished them, not their children, with adoration. For a woman, a muse that doesn't destroy her creativity is an incredible luxury. I realize the importance of falling in love, of passion, in creative development and self-expression. For women this often comes at a cost.

The newcomers to *Baile* I are obvious. They cling to the last row near the wall as desperately as I did the first few months after I moved up from the introductory class. I

remember my own fears upon seeing theirs. It seemed perfectly natural, akin to the experience of ascending through
grades in school. It is important that nothing comes easily.
Each of us must earn our way to the next level, or we simply
leave, because it is more work than pleasure. I am surprised
to be one of the ones who stayed. It's a pleasure to come to
class, and that is all the motivation I need. Many who leave
have talent, but they expect too much from themselves and
burn out. I avoid my old tendency to pursue perfection,
knowing I will never be a professional dancer. I have the
delicious luxury of being able to enjoy myself.

I avoid dancing in the front row and seek the middle.
I am comfortable there. This is odd because in real class-
rooms in my life, I naturally moved to the front of the room,
the front of the class. I identified with being smart and
getting As. I no longer need to be "special" in the old way. I
have nothing to prove. I want to dance. It's that straightfor-
ward. The newer students in the back row follow us. I don't
mind being studied and watched, since I have recently been
doing the same thing. We end up teaching each other. I like
that. Sometimes I crave approval, which is rarely forth-
coming. But even in this, I am not as attached as I might
have been when I was younger. I am much less self-critical
and have less need to attain perfection. The experience of
freedom liberates and invigorates me.

The performing dance company dances in our studio
too. Watching them, we see what is possible before our very
eyes. Dancers in the company also teach, so we quickly
become a community of learners and teachers. Several children dance at my level, including the children of two of the

principal dancers and teachers. They have been dancing since they were *niños*. Flamenco turns out to be a family affair, with children dancing and watching their parents dance. The young ones wear little colored dots on their flamenco shoes to help them distinguish their right from their left. At the annual Christmas show, they perform with the rest of us, often doing short solos that soften our hearts and bring smiles to our faces.

One teacher's son is small for his age. He hides behind his long hair, but he has a handsome face with dark, sparkling eyes. In spite of the fact he hides, he likes to be noticed. One day, I know, he will be a world-renowned flamenco dancer. He comes from generations of flamenco dancers, his great-grandmother having brought flamenco to Albuquerque in the 1930s. He has his father's unerring ease of movement and has been around flamenco since conception. I'll see him perform as an adult and treasure my memories of having danced beside him on the crowded dance floor. I almost stepped on him once, and he started to laugh when I got upset. These kids are strong. Something is being required of them, given to them. They are growing into the challenge and becoming better and better dancers while I slowly move forward. It is as it should be.

By nature, I am reserved. American culture encourages extroversion. Growing up with the children of Chinese immigrants in San Francisco worked well for me. My classmates did not shout or make glaring eye contact or disrespect their teachers with too many questions or inattention. My ability to feel so at ease in the flamenco world surprises me. The hard edges of the Spanish Gypsy culture, like the defined boundaries of the Chinese students, give me a wide berth for my natural introversion. We all have reasons for being in the studio, but all these reasons meet in the center: flamenco. Many of the younger dancers are poor scholarship kids. We have a shared purpose that has nothing to do with age or class or even race. Yet I feel a special kinship with them because I too was a scholarship kid taking modern dance classes in the Telegraph Hill community center in North Beach.

Where is flamenco leading me? The time and effort I am putting into this astounds me. From two half-hour classes a week, I have moved up to three one-hour classes. I have discovered a seemingly insatiable appetite for learning the next sequence of steps. If I miss a class, I fall behind. I am motivated to keep going even though I will never dance in the company, never make it into a career. My desire, then, seems quite inexplicable and fortunate.

Somehow I want to dance, not think about it. Flamenco is about rhythm and expressing the rhythm. Being the rhythm. It keeps me in the moment, moving moment to moment. *I am just doing this until I turn sixty,* I tell myself. *It is a lark, some fun, but nothing serious.*

My sixtieth birthday comes and goes as I move up to *Baile* II. I buy another pair of shoes, this time with professional soles. I get another skirt, less frilly and more practical. Spain creeps into my imagination. Classes are longer now, lasting two hours. Dancing six hours a week elevates my self-confidence and brings me a sense of deep well-being.

I am in love—what more can I say? For me dancing

is like kissing. My first kiss with my first boyfriend on a full-moon night at the ocean. Kisses in my dreams with gentle poets. The hot breath of horses in a paddock against my cheek. Everyday kisses like ice cream and pizza. Taut kisses like cool rain. Distracted kisses first thing in the door. Sad kisses. Comfortable kisses. The new body flaming kisses. Tickle kisses. Pornographic kisses. I-love-you kisses. Married kisses. Affair kisses. Movie-star kisses. And now the flamenco kiss. And I don't have to get married or have an affair, have kids, or turn anything into a career. I delight in the open-ended, always incomplete pleasure that leaves me hungry for more.

Chapter Five
Self-Sovereignty

Women, then, have not had a dog's chance of
writing poetry. That's why I've laid so much
stress on money and a room of one's own.
—Virginia Woolf, *A Room of One's Own*

When have women had a room of their own? Rarely. Even if the whole house was theirs, in the sense that they were in charge of it, they rarely had a room that was just for their use. Women seldom lived independently in their own apartments, houses, or studios. It was the same with money. Husbands controlled the wealth even if they married into it. The only women who controlled their finances were the working-class women who had little time or money to consider the merits of a room of their own.

A few women, such as Vita Sackville-West, a twentieth-century British aristocrat, managed to have the prerequisites necessary for the ideal creative life. Publishing more than fifteen novels and as many books of poetry, Vita lived a rare life for a late Victorian woman. In addition to her enduring marriage, she had many lovers, including Virginia Woolf, who based her fantasy novel *Orlando* on Vita's life. Before her marriage at the age of twenty-one, Vita stood to inherit the largest house in all of England, Knole. Being a woman, she was passed over for the next male heir, a distant relation. Though she would later, after her marriage, acquire a prominent estate of her own, being passed over because of her sex turned her into a gender rebel for the rest of her life.

A room of my own. Why do I keep returning to that after all these years? Why, in spite of the fact that I am writing in a room that is my own unless we have houseguests, do I still crave more space than I have—a more private space? Carolyn Heilbrun writes in her memoir *The Last Gift of Time: Life Beyond Sixty* about buying a house of her own. She was well-off, sharing a home in the country and another in New York City with her family. A married woman with adult children and grandchildren, she craved her own place. In her sixties, after she retired from her academic position at Columbia University, she went house hunting and bought an extremely modern, efficient house for herself.

This tale has an unusual twist. Off she went for her first night. She discovered herself unsettled to a degree. She had, after all, been married for over forty years. When her husband knocked at her door, she was quite relieved to see him standing there. She had never managed completely on her own before. He inquired if he might keep her company. They sat together and read, after he helped her set up a better reading lamp. In a sense, nothing had changed, but in another, everything had changed. She had taken an action, and her husband now was a welcome guest in her house. After marrying young, raising children, and sharing her life, she must have felt an incredible sense of daring and freedom unimagined in her youth.

Women must find out more about these desires. They need to explore the traces of their unlived lives and explore these questions—act on their own behalf. They won't know until they experience the dimensions of their hunger and have their fantasies gratified. For too long they have been ensnared in a double bind: either give up space, be it psychic or physical, and hopefully be accepted and loved, or push for space and be an unwanted "old maid." In the worst case, a woman gives up her life for others, forfeits the opportunity to become self-reliant, and then finds herself adrift after a late divorce or widowhood.

Why can't women have both love and space? Only one of Picasso's many wives and mistresses did. She was singular in her ability to survive Picasso's rejection when he started a quite predictable affair with another woman. All of Picasso's women were artists, but only Francoise Gilot went on to paint and become successful in her own right. When the famous doctor Jonas Salk asked her to marry him, she wrote him a long letter telling him that she would but only under certain conditions. She could live with him for part of the year. She would travel and show her work the other part of the year. She could not give him the kind of companionship most husbands expected from wives. To her surprise, he accepted. And he never went back on his word. Their marriage was extraordinary, bringing them great joy and a feeling of cherishment.

I had the literal experience of a "room of one's own" when I bought a friend's small craftsman some years ago. I fixed it up and went there regularly to write and to sketch. I treasured the bright light and solitude of my little house.

Often, I would arrive and go straight up to the loft and take a nap, surprised at how tired I was from carrying myself in that other world. When I woke up, I would make tea and stare out the window at the rooftops of the old, weathered Victorians. Gradually, I would find my way onto the page. Then it was just timeless flow. I often listened to music. Music, naps, writing, sketching, and an occasional photograph. Staring out the window, I experienced the immense happiness that accompanied my burst of creativity.

I attempted to sleep over a few times, and the experience was always unfortunate. At night, alone, after my good day, I would find myself restless, bored, and homesick. I wanted to return from that green fertile world of my imagination to familiar faces and shared rhythms. I learned how vital both worlds were to my functioning as an artist and a woman. I did not need a room of my own all the time. I just needed it to be there all the time. Now my little house is rented, and I have a room of my own in a converted bedroom in our house. I dearly miss the experience of myself I had in my little house. I haven't figured out how to replace it. It remains, oddly, just out of reach.

Being in the flamenco studio, though, is a close second. I am astounded to experience the same freedom I had alone in my little house. Both places transport me to that special world. The world of marriage, men, children, and domesticity disappears. All the gender-specific parts of my nature disappear. I feel like a boisterous nine-year-old girl again, big and bold and sure of myself, in a world filled with wonder and possibility. I am reconnected to the fourteen-year-old girl who slept under her art table because it took up all the floor space. She listened to Gregorian chants and wrote poetry late into the night. She also, unfortunately, was acutely aware of being twenty pounds overweight, or so she thought.

In the true sense of the word, "virgin" is less a label regarding sexual experience than a matter of self-sovereignty for a woman. That is the symbolic meaning of a room of one's own. It means my body and mind belong to me. The mirror that keeps me guessing, pleasing, coaxing, and nursing others along is gone. Writing the *Canterbury Tales* in the Middle Ages, Geoffrey Chaucer had his Wife of Bath speak for women's desire for the same "sovereignty" in marriage as men. Though the character is called blunt and outspoken, she proclaims her right to be a free person, whether married or not.

I never expected to feel this freedom, this delicious experience of self-sovereignty, in the presence of others. I thought that being truly alone was the critical ingredient. But the presence or absence of people is not the issue. The real issue is what I do in a space and how I feel about myself while I am there. In the studio no one knows me as a mother, wife, teacher, or even writer. I am just another dancer. No questions. This must be the way women who wrote under male pen names felt. They could be bold and creative yet anonymous.

In the dance studio I can explore new personas without offending, appearing unduly self-centered, or losing connection because I am not who others expect me to be. I am not in charge of how things turn out for anyone else. At the center of this process, I discover more space and more inspiration to live a creative life. In flamenco there is the term *ambiente*, which refers to the mood or the atmosphere of such rich environments.

My little house, Virginia Woolf's room, and the flamenco studio all have *ambiente*. Maybe I am too sensitive to the needs and wants of others. Maybe I should have better boundaries like my husband does. I have tried many things to feel better about my need for this kind of freedom. I have also tried many things to eliminate the oppression I feel trying to do creative work when other people are at home. All I know is that when I get what I need in this respect, I am satisfied. The discontent and yearning, even the undercurrents of repressed anger, stop. I blossom. When I return home, I have more energy and vigor to share with my family. I tell myself that I should be able to find this space no matter where I am, that the portal is in me, not a studio. But the truth is, the physical environment does matter.

Carolyn Heilbrun compares the older woman to King Lear. When people divest themselves of their gender roles, the outcome is not the same for women as for men, with each forfeiting unique powers. For men, these classical roles often related to productive work and economic power, whereas for women, their gender roles stressed beauty and reproductive capacity. Instead of feeling cheated, stripped, and useless, if they are smart and fortunate, women can enter a period of wonderful freedoms. No longer objects to be admired and sexualized, no longer encompassed by their maternal patterns, they can do as they please if they have the means, the courage, and the energy left for it.

My grandmothers and my mother didn't succeed in this. My maternal grandmother died in early menopause, while the other died of "old age" at sixty-seven. My mother tried to find her power, her voice, and her freedom, but she damaged her health by smoking too much too long. She died at the same "old age" as my father's mother, which thirty years later was considered too young. I am the first woman in my family to have such a chance to know this kind of freedom. This realization surprises me and fills me with gratitude. I'd be a fool not to make the most of this singular gift.

Awareness of time's passage wakes me in the middle of the night. I know a time of dissolution awaits, like the waxing moon. Dancing flamenco, I embrace the inevitable variety of moods that intimations of mortality bring. Like the stages of grief that Elisabeth Kübler-Ross describes, sometimes I am in denial. Sometimes I bargain. Sometimes I rage. And sometimes I surrender. The winds of inspiration and creativity guide me. I remind myself to let go of attachment to "outcomes," as the Buddhists teach. I don't know where my desire will lead or how long it will last. It is such a relief not to struggle for an answer. All I need to do is show up for my truth, and the rest will take care of itself.

In Jason Weber's memoir about his time in Spain, he observes that flamenco is an art form that expresses the anguish not just of love lost, as in the blues or in country-western music, but of the ever-present reality of death itself. Time can't be stopped. Aging can't be stopped. At the heart of flamenco is a lament, a special kind of love song to the reality of impermanence. The origins of flamenco go back and back, mapping the spirit of many peoples who struggled against poverty, oppression, exile, and persecution.

Musical influences of the Gypsies, the Moors, the Arabs, the Jews, and the Andalusians of southern Spain combine to give flamenco its depth and power of emotion. Flamenco celebrates life while it protests inevitable death. There is no time like the present. What are you waiting for? Stand up and be counted. It's your one and only life, after all!

Chapter Six
Mythic Realities

In that moment, his spirit came alive. He felt a unison
with the power of the bull, and with the grace and
beauty of the eagle. He felt the inspirations of his
creative life coming together. He felt his inner dance.
—Teo Morca

My father died when I was one, and I don't remember
anything about his illness or his death. I grew up
and learned to walk and to speak in the emotional waters
of my mother's grief. My experiences following my father's
premature death and having few close relatives who lived
into their eighties have had an unexpected benefit. I treasure every moment of health and freedom. My husband
has had the opposite experience. I used to envy the fact
that his parents, still alive into their nineties, live vital and
independent lives. Now, as we enter our sixties, I am not as
sure. He seems less able to seize this extraordinary time,
sounding on occasion as if the best of life is behind him.

I blame my family's mortality patterns on ancestral bad
habits, with smoking and drinking at the top of the list. My
mother and I often debated this subject with some heat.
Since her own mother, an old-world Catholic, had never
smoked or drank and still had not lived to see her fiftieth

birthday, my mother smoked and drank with some impunity. This did indeed shorten her life considerably. Bad habits can shorten a life, but good habits don't ensure longevity. As with all matters of faith, I am an agnostic. I just don't know, so I do all I can to hedge my bets. Fortunately, I actually enjoy eating the right kinds of food and getting regular exercise. I just feel better, no matter how long I might live. This factor was at the center of my arguments with my mother. She said she enjoyed her habits, "thank you very much."

I do know that death is an ironic trickster who slides through rooms like a warm breeze, eating late-fall apples and burping cider. Sometimes death sends cold blasts in spring after days of warmth have encouraged the fruit trees to bloom too early. Other times, death invites us to dip our feet in the shallows, where little fish nibble our toes before gobbling us up whole, and calls it play. Death is notoriously capricious. Death is the red color of blood meeting air, of life lived with passion. Death is our birthright and our completion, utterly natural and utterly inevitable.

The stances of the bullfighter and the flamenco dancer evoke the spirit of *duende*. Both begin their "performance" in stark stillness, with their faces devoid of expression. Concentrated energy flows upward to the sky and spirals downward into the earth as the *toreador* or *bailaora* prepares for motion. Arms raised high overhead, feet firmly planted, back arched, head lifted, the bullfighter and the flamenco dancer pull into themselves like a giant wave before going out to meet the potent, mysterious shores of creation. Some of the women who dance in the studio are in remission from various forms of cancer. Some who danced here previously died knowing they had spent their last precious hours joyously. Others who dance here are healthy and carefree.

The perils of existence lurk in spite of all our advances in medicine. Ironically, the more we extend life, the greater the threat becomes of mass extinction. I read in the *Albuquerque Journal* that scientists at Los Alamos, who have been setting the nuclear clock for thirty years, have moved the hand forward. We are now five minutes before twelve because nuclear weapons slip into countries with unstable regimes at an alarming rate. The world has always been filled with war and disease, famine and death. Yet we still are tempted to hide out in numbing routines and put on our happy faces. Or we just sit in our stupor of despair, staring at TV and computer screens.

In spite of everything, you soldier on and pretend to be fine. "How's it going?" the clerk asks as she scans your groceries. You know your day has got to be better than hers. In spite of her degree in art or history, she finds herself standing at a machine, swiping bar codes over and over and over. So you say, "Great, fine," or something like that. Then you ask, "And you? How is your day?" And she may or may not look up as she says, "Good, fine. Can't complain."

If we can't fake it, we take various forms of antidepressants to keep going. Perhaps music and dance are the most ancient antidepressants of all. Flamenco captures the longing of Debussy, the drama of Beethoven, and the wail of a Jewish cantor. It has the sweet, heart rhythms of the blues and the hypnotic, circular patterns of Indian music.

Whatever emotion I have finds expression in flamenco. When I dance, I can grieve and in that grief find the most surprising fullness of life. Oh, what beauty and joy! What rage and anguish, knowing that everything will be lost in time. In these moments I feel closest to life's richness, capable and generous and free.

Through spring to late fall, the back door of the studio opens to an alley, and the expansive New Mexico sky frames the modest downtown skyline. Lavish sunsets turn the world outside that doorway into a place of uncommon holiness. I dance the sundown as currents of cooling air meet my moist skin. It is impossible to dance without sweating. The moment I break into a sweat is often the first moment I have the sensation of strength and well-being that brings me back to class again and again. We try to stay cool, physically and metaphorically, far too often. Native Americans with their sweat lodges and Scandinavians with their saunas know the importance of the physical and emotional release that comes with breaking a good sweat.

Like the dawn, sunsets have potent magic. The transition between day and night is a good time to be on the dance floor. If I have seen a homeless man begging for change under an underpass on my drive to the studio, I dance his poverty. If I have witnessed the image of a dying woman in Haiti with her little girl sitting beside her on the news, I dance that suffering. Nothing is left out, excluded, rejected. All the people in the streets, in the jails, in the ghettos, and in exile are part of me when I dance. Flamenco humanizes me.

In Teo Morca's book *Flamenco Spirit*, he describes his

wife's death in his arms during a rehearsal. It was a haunting tragedy. Yet as I read the story, I also think, *What a beautiful death, to die in the arms of someone who loves you while doing the thing that you love to do.* Not many people have that. So many die alone, in fear, and in pain. Others pass in institutions after long periods of decline. But the bullfighter, like the Japanese samurai, risks his life and paradoxically becomes more alive. The audience vicariously watches, breathless with anticipation, as the human being and the bull size one another up in the ring.

I never understood or tried to understand bullfighting or Spain's long love affair with it. I judged it as a cruel, wrongheaded, male-dominated sport. I still have no interest in going to a fight, but I no longer dismiss what has been part of human culture in societies all over the world. What ritual enactment lies behind this all-too-often mindless spectator sport? Why is the bull so prominent and so sacred in myths and legends? Why did bullfighting fascinate artists like Picasso and Hemingway? As I studied flamenco, and especially when I finally went to Spain, I realized the influence of bullfighting on flamenco.

If I knew I had two days left to live before I would die an accidental death, I would dance and spend time with people I love. I would stare at the sky and watch for birds. I would admire colors and shapes and sounds. I would not count my money or polish my furniture. I would not catch up on the news. Time is precious and finite. We are born, and if lucky, we grow old and die. We suffer. Some have it easier than others, but everyone ends up the same way: dead and eventually forgotten. And while I am here, I will protest. I will let the fullness of existence flow through me. I will dance in front of the mythic bull. I have no desire to hurt or slay him. I honor him with my resistance. He wakes me up and reminds me that this is my life!

So where is flamenco taking me? It can't become a career. I'm too old. I never expected to continue past sixty. Maybe I won't give it up! Children are becoming virtuosos at younger and younger ages. So why not achieve new things at this stage of living? It's nothing I set out to do. Finding flamenco, something that engages all aspects of my being, has me pressing against the limits of what I thought possible. My preconceptions about age scatter like butterflies.

When I finally traveled to Spain, I returned with a vision of a black bull, so black that his coat shone blue in the sunlight. I read every myth and legend about bulls I could find and discovered them to be universal. One day I walked into an art gallery and saw a silk-screen print of the exact bull I had envisioned. The artist was there that day to tell me a story. Since childhood, he had always wanted to run with the bulls in Spain. On his fiftieth birthday he had finally realized his dream.

The print was of the bull he had run with that day. Both the artist and the bull were named Fermin. I bought the picture and hung it over my desk to remind me of the importance of intuition and following one's call. A short time later, I learned the artist had died in a car accident on his way to see family in Los Angeles. Strange synchronicity accompanies such a journey as the permeable borders between myth and reality coax us into new appreciation for life's unfolding. These incidents can illuminate the way. Now when I look at the picture, I think of that day when the artist told me his story: he ran with the bulls, and he lived his dream.

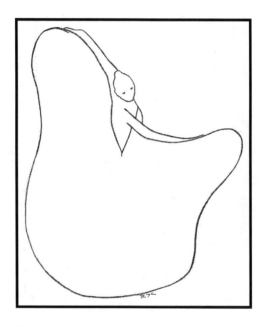

Chapter Seven
Writing and Flamenco

From wonder into wonder, existence opens.
—Lao Tzu

I decided to cut flamenco classes for a week mid-semester to go on a writing retreat in Taos. I have left home for short periods to write but never in such a structured setting. Often, the first precious day or two passes in a muddle. I have considered attempting a silent retreat, but my forays into silent group meditations have been cautionary. Sitting still for long periods of time with groups of strangers, even at a symphony, feels like punishment. I have thought about yoga retreats with more enthusiasm, but they are expensive and layered in social dynamics that I leave home to shed.

Since starting flamenco, I have rarely missed class. Learning the dances requires showing up or falling behind. Falling behind kills motivation. If I have missed class, it has been due to promises to other people, unavoidable responsibilities and duties. Yet something is shifting. Occasionally, I force myself to class without my usual anticipation. Am I losing my beloved muse? I repress a sense of dread. I try not to hide from it or react to it. I try to wait patiently until I know what to do. Am I without direction, in the creative ferment again?

I remind myself that flamenco has taught me to trust myself. Why shouldn't creativity have a natural cycle like the seasons or the waning and waxing of the moon? Still, I resist dissolution, flagging energy, and ebbing desire. The professional-level classes demand more and more time and energy. Getting better and better, I confront obstacles that come with progress, mainly self-criticism. I persevere, but some of the joy of being a beginner has faded. Maybe that joy is like the first high that comes with falling in love, the lure to get you started and keep you going long enough to become seriously attached. Oddly enough, the days I have the most resistance to going to class are the times I experience the most improvement.

In a performance-based school, each level prepares students for the next, leading eventually to the company and the stage. No dillydallying! After painful rumination, I decide to move back to a less demanding, intermediate level. I give myself license to "age-evolve," to set my own pace. Having few expectations, even in this fast-paced and sometimes aggressive curriculum, is part of my pleasure in learning flamenco. Even with my new resolve, thoughts of failure start to nag me. How many things did I give up too soon because I was afraid of not being good enough? How many things did I give up because I forced myself to be good enough and lost the fun?

Going on the writing retreat will allow me to take a break from flamenco. Maybe a new perspective will guide me to the next step, much like how Lao Tzu follows wonder after wonder, trusting. Maybe it is a crazy notion, but I am starting to believe this path he calls "the way" has merit.

The prospect of staying in Mabel Dodge Luhan's house in Taos is a big part of why I am going. Even if the retreat disappoints, I will have a week in a historically complex and architecturally rich house that will reconnect me with my interest in D. H. Lawrence. This is an opportunity to see the windows he painted in Mabel and Tony's bathroom and the second floor of the main house.

I have traveled to Taos many times over the years, to visit Lawrence Ranch a few miles north in San Cristobal. Mabel Dodge Luhan, D. H. Lawrence's wealthy patron, gave it to the Lawrences when the pink adobe house she offered them on her property proved unsatisfactory. Lawrence's wife, Frieda, refused to let Mabel have such ready access to her husband. So to entice them to stay in New Mexico, Mabel gave them the ranch, which Frieda and Lawrence then lived in together briefly but always considered their one true home. After Lawrence's death, Frieda returned to it with her Italian lover, Angelo Ravagli.

Supposedly, Lawrence is buried there in a twelve-by-fifteen foot memorial building, his ashes mixed into the concrete memorial stone beneath the altar. On the altar stands a plaster statue of a phoenix below a round glass window with a hand-painted sunflower by the painter Dorothy Brett. The phoenix, Lawrence's favorite symbol for regeneration, now heralds his immortality. This strange bird figures in myths and legends in many cultures, representing long life and the creative act of destruction that prefigures a renewed cycle of life. Often called a sacred firebird, the phoenix lives up to one thousand years. When the cycle completes, the creature gives itself up in its nest of flames, sacrificing the old worn-out self for rebirth.

One account I read denies that Lawrence's ashes are actually in the memorial stone. Lawrence died in France, and his wife Frieda asked her Italian lover to disinter Lawrence's ashes in Vence, France, and bring them when he came from Italy to live with her at the ranch. According to this account, Angelo—a married man who had left behind a wife and children to whom he would return twenty years later, after Frieda's death—got drunk on the crossing and tossed what was left of his "rival" into the Atlantic. When the boat landed, probably sober and contrite, he substituted sand for ash, and no one knew the difference for quite a while— probably until he drank too much again and boasted of the feat. This story would have amused Lawrence, ever on the side of the passionate, spontaneous response.

Mabel opposed the shrine and boycotted the memorial Frieda held for him. Lawrence, she believed, would have opposed such a thing! How awful to have him memorialized in one spot, as if his free spirit could be contained. Lawrence, I can imagine, would have applauded that too– the heat of the battle between rivals for his affection, the clash of wills. How alive! Of course, Frieda prevailed, but not before Mabel had her protest.

The walk from the house to the shrine meanders through a pine forest. For a man who never settled anywhere in his short lifetime and lived in a permanent state of exile, this enchanted place in what he considered "the new world" allows people to visit and pay homage. Nature writer, social critic, and visionary, Lawrence advocated a kind of human tenderness and vital connection that was antithetical to pornography or money-based relationships. Though he wrote over one hundred years ago, he wouldn't have been surprised at sexting and other forms of what he called "mental sex." He believed that the destruction of the environment was inseparable from what has come to be seen as the "battle of the sexes." I savor the fresh scent of the pines and feel the clear intensity that often comes with high altitudes and a singular purpose. Deep gratitude for this idiosyncratic, working-class British writer permeates my senses.

Inside the shrine, fortune cookies, pens, poems, feathers, and rocks litter the altar. People from all over the world have signed the date book beside the entrance, writing whimsical things. Poems, favorite quotations, and short descriptions follow their names and addresses. Someone has written out a short verse from Lawrence's last poem, "The Ship of Death," in black ink and placed it at the foot of the phoenix.

> Oh build your ship of death, your little ark
> And furnish it with food, with little cakes and wine
> For the dark flight down oblivion.

To the left of the poem stands an empty wine glass beside a fruit cake still in its red cellophane wrapping. Here it is: the ironic, the sacred, the spontaneous. In the face of impending "oblivion," Lawrence's vision of life animates his poems, short stories, essays, and novels. I smile.

Many accounts circulate of Lawrence's dark moods,

scathing tongue, and chronic irritability. In poor health and living with his wife in semi-poverty, he pushed himself to keep moving, keep writing, and keep living. He often raged about the state of the world. Yet he loved the intimate details of the natural world and the small rituals of daily existence.

He imagined a world without greed and lamented the destruction of the human capacity for tenderness. He drew inspiration from the "trembling balance" of nature. Growing up the son of a coal miner in Nottingham, England, in the late 1890s, he witnessed the effects of industrialization, including the destruction of the countryside and dehumanization of the workers. Living through World War I, he struggled against the forces of death that seemed to doom Europe. Yet in his final poem, "The Ship of Death," his humanity and his love of life triumph over cynicism.

Like many others, I too had written short responses in the date book and offered tokens of homage at his shrine. During my years of research and writing about Lawrence, however, I hadn't focused on the women around Lawrence, especially not the Taos patron of the arts Mabel Dodge Luhan. At my retreat, in the little bookstore at the bottom of the staircase leading up to the second-floor bedrooms, I bought a volume of Mabel's autobiography and discovered a wonderful writer. Mabel's autobiography spans four volumes, documenting her transformation from New York heiress to Florentine princess to a woman in the new world.

Mabel describes her flock of pigeons in the opening pages in *Winter in Taos*. The precise, rich details of her extraordinary ordinary life in the house she built with Tony, a Native American from the Taos Pueblo, opens a deeply personal and feminine world that had been missing in my professional studies. In the book, Mabel tells of a Chicago art dealer who visited her in the 1920s and fancied her sign requesting, "Please don't drive in. The pigeons don't like it." Refusing his offer to buy the sign, she wondered what gave him, living in a large city, "the unfailing feeling of wonder and bliss that pigeons thrill one with year after year." During breaks between eating, doing yoga, and writing, I sit on the front porch and watch the remnants of her flock come and go.

Mabel made several false starts before finding Taos and settling there for the rest of her life. Her story reminds me that there is always a risk of failure when following one's muse. The gap between fantasy and experience has created some strange landings for me. I often dreamed of living in a quaint village in England, perhaps near a picturesque local cemetery. When I lived in Northern California, I wanted to live in Ferndale, a small Victorian town with a true old-world cemetery.

On a rolling hill ending in stands of ancient redwoods, the Ferndale cemetery is filled with ornate and well-maintained tombstones, many of them situated in plots for families of Danish or Portuguese descent. I fell in love, instantly, with a two-story Victorian house that backed the cemetery. Once the rectory, it had belonged to the church next to it. An artist inhabited the church, using it for both home and studio. Another artist and her husband lived in the adjacent house, painted dusty rose and boasting flower gardens and raised beds with vegetables in the back. I found sweet romance in the way the vegetables bordered the cemetery, life and death in one line of vision.

Both properties were for sale. The artist living in the church urged me to buy his, saying it was a much better deal, but I wanted the pink house, pure and simple. How I wanted it, and how it wanted me! From the bedroom on the second story, I looked out over the graveyard toward a stand of redwoods at the crest of the hill. I imagined watching the herons fly in at dusk, settling like luminous crosses in the darkening boughs of the old trees. But my husband said quite emphatically, "I will never live in this house." Whatever spirit or ghost that beckoned me repulsed him. I later found out it was indeed haunted. Ghosts either want you in their space, or they don't. This ghost had a real thing for me, because my longing for the house nearly broke up my relationship.

We bought a different house, one we both could love. A few years later, I rented a room at the bed and breakfast around the corner from my pink house with views of the graveyard. I stayed in the Heron Room. *Perfect*, I thought. It was a curious summer. Usually, Humboldt County is shrouded in fog and mist in July, especially Ferndale with its proximity to the ocean. But that August broke heat records. My room, with its heavy Victorian furniture and rugs, was hot and stuffy though the windows were open wide. I unpacked and then got my notebook and went across the street to the cemetery.

I walked the narrow meandering paths between the carved granite tombstones that first evening, hoping for inspiration. But a foul order, faint at first, steadily increased as I made my way up the hill toward the tree line for a better view of the town. The only smell I could compare it to was the smell of sewer gas that had once flooded a bathroom in a house I rented during college. When I returned to the inn and told the owners, they nodded. The water table was a problem. The coffins often lifted up, touching the surface, and had to be pressed back down. What I had smelled that hot day was the stench of decomposing bodies. Real bodies, not the vague romantic visions in the fantasies that had brought me there.

In my second winter in New Mexico, I rented an adobe *casita* from a painter friend. It was the original house, over one hundred years old. As I drove to Taos, the leaden skies, the freezing cold, and the muddy, rutted roads sank my mood. The room was small with low ceilings. Tiny recessed windows let in little light. A couch folded out into a bed. A pine desk with a lamp was the only bright spot. I unpacked my things and looked around. I opened the door to a blast of freezing cold and a view of a muddy, rutted lane. Too cold, too small, too dark. Once again, I felt like Goldilocks in "Goldilocks and the Three Bears," searching for the right bowl of porridge, the right chair, and the right bed.

I made a cup of tea in the closet of a kitchen and thought, *What shall I do?* I forced myself to read and write until night. Bad dreams disturbed my sleep. I woke up to an indefinable sense of menace. I lasted two days before I gave up and drove home, each mile away from Taos bringing me increasing relief. I chastised myself. What had I been thinking? What was I looking for that kept leading me into various stages of shock, if not horror? Was I simply an incurable, delusional romantic? Later, reading Mabel's autobiography, I realized that risk and failure were natural parts of the process of making one's life an authentic experience.

When I returned from my retreat, I decided to accept a time of uncertainty. In the past I would have given up flamenco, justifying the decision in many ways. I wanted a different process this time, one that felt like completion, not failure. After years of persistent and steady work, did I just give it up? What would allow me to move into the next thing with something distilled, honored, flowered? The new course of study forced us to learn castanets and to participate in *cuadro* class, two aspects of flamenco I had resisted.

No longer "enchanted," I became a better dancer. I knew how to appreciate and understand flamenco. I was almost able to craft my own dance. I had rationalized my reluctance to take *cuadro* classes to learn how to perform a solo dance under the umbrella of "I don't want to be a performer. I am dancing for myself." Yet I knew something rang false because I was scared, painfully self-conscious. My perfectionism had plagued me in all areas of creative self-expression. Old fundamental patterns of insecurity blocked me every time. Usually, I interpreted the obstacle as lack of talent or interest. My path through flamenco, however, challenged this interpretation because I loved it so much. My love, so far, was stronger than my familiar self-doubt.

So what is *cuadro*? It is where all the hours of study lead. Students stand in a circle doing *palmas*, a rhythmic hand clapping. One student at a time breaks into the circle and dances a piece uniquely her own. Some people can't get enough of the feeling of being seen, dancing their dance. Others pull back as if they might drown, the empty circle like an ocean. I know from experience that forcing myself into the terrifying water just to prove I can won't produce good results. Some things can't be exacted.

I wasn't on the hero's journey that Joseph Campbell describes in *A Hero with A Thousand Faces* but more on the un-journey of Lao Tzu, the ancient Chinese philosopher. Forcing things, forcing myself, simply shut doors for me. Yet how could I overcome the tenacious obstacle of my own disinclination and fear? How could I trust myself enough to follow my intuition? How many doors had failed to open because of this internal confusion and indecision? Still, I balked at this singular opportunity.

I was at the edge, again, of my limitations. Craft my own dance, write my own poem, sing my own song, live my own life? That lust for independence again. I kept finding it over and over in different contexts. I could always get As in school and do what was expected, but I panicked when I asked myself, *What am I doing this for?* For external validation? That never worked for long. The end result of that course was emptiness, hunger, and more heroic drive. I longed for another way, a less competitive way. I couldn't memorize my path into my song. I had to find it within. But how?

Authenticity and *duende* are inseparable—being true and revealed. Honest. I was attracted and terrified. Practice and study could only take me so far. I envied the little girl of one of the dancers for her lack of self-consciousness. She followed her mother into class with a direct, confident expression. Though she sat on the benches behind us, she participated. She dressed up to come to class, wearing colorful skirts, bright socks, and party shoes. Her hair in pigtails framed her moon-shaped face and intelligent almond-shaped eyes. She never whined or seemed bored the way other children forced to sit through class did. Humming to herself, clapping to the rhythms, she would buckle and unbuckle her shoes, take off her socks, then put them on again. Her rich inner world glowed like a halo around her.

One thing leads to another. As the old Chinese scholar says, "existence opens." Five years of dance had led to my first retreat, to doing yoga, and to writing in Mabel Dodge Luhan's supportive environment. A week before the March retreat, my daughter had been in Japan during the earthquake and tsunami and nuclear reactor meltdown. My schizophrenic son, a poet, was off his meds and back in jail. The obstacles of this time, of this time of life, seemed to be increasing. New caretaking responsibilities and inevitable losses signaled the shift into the category of "elderly." There were so many reasons to cancel or decline dates with my muse, yet the press of limited time impelled me not to.

A flame of new life. Lawrence's phoenix rising from the ashes of the gone before. On the last day of my writer's retreat, I linger on the grounds of Mabel's house. I laugh, once more, at the sight of a few pigeons still roosting in what Mabel called their "Mexican village." I wonder why the flock has thinned so drastically. Even in their somewhat dilapidated state, the high wooden birdhouses stacked close upon one another in imprecise, organic unity still seem ideal for breeding. But the pigeons know that was then and this is now, and the flock, like time, moves on.

I return to the main house. Its homey elegance fills me with a sense of domestic contentment. On the adobe walls hang photographs of Mabel with her bangs and pageboy haircut and Tony wrapped in a white blanket with an inscrutable expression on his face. Georgia O'Keefe paintings adorn the walls, and first-edition books by famous authors who have dined in these very rooms fill the bookshelves. Nooks with chairs and sofas invite reading and lounging and intimate conversation. I have never been in a place where creativity and domesticity strike this delightful balance.

Before I drive home, I walk the labyrinth at the edge of the property where Pueblo land and Mabel's land join. After entering the maze, I realize I don't have an offering to place in the center, with the pennies, the dice, the cards, and the flowers. I gather two fallen twigs from the path to place in a cross in the center, marking this time of crossroads. The center holds the wishes, the intentions, and the realizations of the many who have come this far. I offer mine and say yes, my heart open with joy and wonder. Leaving, I start to hurry. An inner voice reminds me that how I leave is as important as how I entered. I walk slowly and pay attention. In front of one of the clusters of low adobe houses to my right, drying laundry blows in a gentle wind like prayer flags.

I drive a few blocks and park illegally close to the Kit

Carson Cemetery to pay a last homage to Mabel. On her gravestone, I place a handmade sugar skull with sequin eyes, a gift from my sister when she visited at Halloween. Earlier in the week, during one of our afternoon breaks, I explored the cemetery to find Mabel's grave. Teenagers ditching school smoked under one of the old cottonwoods. A young couple with a toddler in diapers sat under a tree, talking in quiet tones while the little girl stumbled through the grass. It took two complete turns around the circular paths of the small graveyard to find Mabel's modest tombstone tucked in one corner. No carved angels or fine words for her. No more architectural exhibitions of her persona.

Modest and simple, almost Zen-like except for the tokens of esteem decorating it, her grave is easy to overlook. I appreciate this contrast. She lived a complete life filled with all the trappings of wealth and imagination. Then she was done. The Taos Pueblo Indians retrieved Tony after his death, less than a year after Mabel's death, and took his body back to their land. Mabel did not return to her blueblood East Coast ancestral burial grounds. She stayed with the place she had found on the border between worlds and left behind her legacy of a privileged and creative woman's life in her memoirs and her house.

What is *duende*? What is its opposite? Where is the middle? I think about how to find that magical place between the inner and the outer, between duty and calling. Each person has a unique relationship to this juncture. Mabel lived a series of *duendes* expressed in houses and lifestyles. She lived out her dreams, yet she was criticized for a lack of "originality." I disagree. She was a visionary homemaker, a builder of new worlds, and a true patron of the arts. She searched for a domestic way of life that embodied her vision of life's creative possibilities. A seeker, she traveled the world until she found her place, Taos, New Mexico, and her love, Tony Luhan. Her magic was the finding of place.

What is *duende?* How do we express it? Live it? How do we respond or not respond, and what are the consequences? Was Tony's expression of *duende* crossing the divide between the Pueblo and the white man's worlds to beat a drum under Mabel's window? Was *duende* Mabel's daring to marry Tony and live in their sprawling adobe house on the border of two worlds? Was it the painter Dorothy Brett's repudiation of her British aristocratic background and her devotion to D. H. Lawrence? Was it Frieda Lawrence's sacrifice of her economic privilege, home, and family to marry Lawrence and join him in his search for a new way of life? One thing I believe for sure is that *duende* moves us forward, takes us to the next step. It can't be faked, rushed, or bought. And you know when it happens.

Chapter Eight
Ancestral Traces

A fisherman acknowledges his family,
"aumakua," the shark, before casting his net.
—M. J. Harden, *Voices of Wisdom: Hawaiian Elders Speak*

I went to a zazen meditation instruction recently, and the monk had us do an exercise. We brought our hands in front of our face, palms together, then moved them apart to the sides of our heads. The monk said, "The left hand is your past, and the right hand is your future. Where are they?" Then the monk said, "Bring your palms back together. Now be with this." I experienced a simple feeling of an embodied moment that was miraculously empty and full at the same time. This same sense of being alive in the moment flourishes when I dance flamenco. Ancestral memory textures moments that often fill me with love, gratitude, and a sense of loss. I am alive in this moment, while many others lived, loved, struggled, and died. Their invisible presence, for better or worse, hums in my bones.

On my last trip to Hawaii, I bought a book called *Voices of Wisdom: Hawaiian Elders Speak*. Reading the interviews with the elders and looking closely at their radiant, open faces, I realized my grandfather's spirit in my life. Born in Honolulu to Portuguese immigrants in the late 1880s, he grew up immersed in the renaissance of Hawaiian culture. His father, my great-grandfather, built a generous, three-story house for his ten children. The family prospered in a brief period of economic stability and growth for the natives and the immigrants. They were the lucky ones.

Grandpa Borges's family came from an area in Portugal near the Spanish border. I don't know how long they lived there before fleeing to the Azores, small islands in the Atlantic. I guess the Azores provided a temporary resting place during forced migrations. People searching for work braved the seas to work for the growing pineapple and sugar industries in Hawaii. The Japanese and the Portuguese arrived around the same time. The Japanese men came alone, working the fields and living together in tenements. The Portuguese brought their families and managed to set up house, experiencing less discrimination and isolation than their Asian counterparts. For the most part, the early Portuguese immigrants multiplied and prospered.

Grandpa Borges and my father were musicians. Grandpa grew up around amazing Hawaiian singers, dancers, and musicians. My father played the piano, and my grandfather played the slide guitar and the ukulele. Three Portuguese cabinetmakers from Madeira built the first ukuleles in Hawaii in the late 1880s. The instrument was quickly assimilated into the high culture of Hawaiian music. King Kalahaua reportedly included ukulele music in his royal concerts, his patronage making the instrument part of Hawaiian compositions and fusing the best of two worlds.

On my first trip to Portugal, I visited the town Castelo

de Vide, my great-grandfather's birthplace. This walled medieval city sits above vast expanses of well-tended, rolling farmlands. When the Romans came through centuries earlier, they constructed fountains throughout the city to tap the natural underground springs. This legendary water entices people from all over Europe to the spa built in one corner of the town. Some legends have it that the fountain of youth resides here. When I visited, most of the people on the streets were old; maybe the fountain of youth simply means the fountain of longevity.

Narrow cobblestone streets meander into little parks, each with a constantly flowing, ancient fountain. I watched people come and fill their jugs and move quietly back to their houses. I wondered if the water contained lithium because many of the town's residents just sat in the parks calmly, doing nothing at all. Everyone in the town moved slowly, as if practicing walking meditation. No one hurried. The old men with olive complexions wore traditional-looking clothing: little back hats, black pants, and vests. Some of them still rode on horse-driven carts down the narrow streets and the country lanes leaving the city.

These small-boned, compact men reminded me of Grandpa Borges. They had the same tranquil air too. But he wore pin-striped suits, wide ties with bright colors, and wide-brimmed felt hats pulled down on one side like men in the "old classics" movies. My mother used to say with some amazement that my grandfather weighed 130 pounds "soaking wet." Completely bald, his head was perfectly shaped, and his ears were perfect too, like seashells. My mother said I had his head and ears. She was jealous because her ears stuck out, and she hated that so much that for a while she glued them back.

Grandpa Borges was different somehow. I wonder why my grandmother, a third-generation Californian from a Scottish-Irish background, married him. My guess is she fell for his music and his looks. She loved to play the piano herself. The black sheep in her family, she could have been quite a party girl. Probably, on one of their dates, he brought her to a family luau, and she fell in love with a sense of beauty, ease, and freedom she had never experienced before. She might not have liked other things about his culture, but she embraced the luau with an open heart. Whenever Grandpa Borges had time off, he had a quasi luau in their backyard, eating and drinking and making music with family and a few friends.

Grandpa Borges worked for the state of California. Because of his slight build, he was chosen to paint the inner towers of the Golden Gate Bridge. The painters would start on one side, and by the time they got to the other side, it would be time to go back and start all over. It was a life's work. Whenever I drive over the Golden Gate, I look up and picture his life high above the ocean, with views of San Francisco on one side and the open seas on the other. I imagine he sang his songs to the wind, sending them home to Hawaii as he dipped his brush in a bucket of rust-resistant orange paint.

I was six when he died in the middle of the night from a heart attack. Just like that, he was gone. During that time people didn't really talk much about death with their children. No grief counseling for us. Yet I still remember being in their backyard in the cushioned, shaded swinging couch. Everything felt just right. Sometimes I would take a nap, my head in my mother's or my grandmother's lap. And flowers, especially my grandmother's roses, perfumed the air. I didn't know I was living in another culture that prized music and community and nature more than anything else. Sometimes we would go over to my cousins' house for a big luau when people from the islands came to visit the mainland. Then more musicians and singers would come. There would be hula dancing too, in real grass skirts. It was the Hawaiian way.

When I visited New Zealand a few years ago and heard the Maori sing, I felt my grandfather's presence. The Maori have angels in their voices. Such a heavenly beauty. It must have something to do with being part of the islands and the sea. I hadn't expected to hear the love in my grandfather's voice coming to me through the body of a heavyset, tattooed Maori. At funerals, everyone in the Maori culture has to sing. It doesn't matter what you sing, but you sing. Everyone shares the heart's expression through his or her voice. I understand this. It feels right to me because of my grandfather.

I just knew, somehow, that Grandma and Grandpa didn't have an easy marriage. They never fought in my presence, but my grandfather stayed out of my grandmother's way. Grandma was the rebellious one in her family, and my grandfather was her one lifelong rebellion against the grim Protestant values she had endured as a child (spare the rod and spoil the child). I have a picture of her with her whole family, all ten sisters standing behind their mother and father. The picture was taken in front of the big white house my great-grandfather built in Claremont, California. My great-grandmother's gray hair is pulled straight back. She is wearing a white blouse buttoned to her throat and a floor-length black skirt with an apron. She is thin and stands ramrod straight, and her mouth turns down at the corners. I can't imagine anyone curling up on her lap. I can't imagine her dancing or drinking or marrying a Portuguese man. My great-grandfather has the same grim, determined expression. They remind me of the painting *American Gothic* by Grant Wood.

My grandmother's father ruled the all-woman clan with an iron hand. One of his daughters, my great-aunt Myrtle, left her husband the first time he hit her. She said she had grown up with that and wasn't going to take it when she had a choice. I admired her brave spirit. I never loved my grandmother, though. Maybe life had been a big disappointment, and she didn't care about anyone after my father, her only child, died. And that was the only time in which I could remember her, after his death. She just lived in a hazy place far away inside of herself. She made my clothes and spent time with me, but it was like being with a ghost. I didn't trust her, either. Maybe she was an alcoholic and always in a half-drunk state. Whatever the reason, I avoided her whenever I could. She seemed to live in a shadow even when she was standing in the sunshine.

My mother and my grandmother had a long-standing feud too. I think my grandmother resented my mother for getting pregnant too soon and maybe even blamed her, irrationally, for my father's untimely death. Even so, my mother maintained contact with her until she died in a nursing home. I remember visiting Grandma after her stroke. My mother would wheel her outside and let her smoke a cigarette or eat chocolates, both things forbidden by the staff. Watching my grandma stuff chocolates into her mouth made me sad, and I wanted to run away from her when she would ask for a kiss before we left. Visiting her in that nursing home made me afraid of growing old. Nursing homes in those days could be pretty bad.

Grandpa Borges had once tried to leave my grand-mother for another woman. My grandmother, the larger of the two of them, found out and threw him down the stairs. He never left her for the other woman, so I suppose he was too afraid or resigned. They had worked things out by the time I was born. Grandpa Borges ate his meals at a Formica table on the sunporch at the back of the house. He didn't eat "normal" food, but I preferred it. While Grandma and my mother and great-aunts ate meat, potatoes, and gravy in the dining room, I ate rice and fish and steamed vegetables with my grandpa. He taught me how to eat with chopsticks and to use just the right amount of soya sauce.

Grandpa Borges might have been Jewish. That would account for his curious isolation. I discovered an old Jewish enclave in Castelo de Vide. Perhaps the Spanish Inquisition had sent my grandfather's family scrambling for their lives from Spain. After a while, Portugal had become inhospi-table too. They all had to keep going, first to the Azores and then to where job prospects were better, Hawaii in the late 1800s. I wonder if when my great-grandfather and great-grandmother got off the boat, they looked around and thought they had died and gone straight to heaven. I'll bet they vowed right there on the spot to put down roots and stay the rest of their days.

My Portuguese great-grandfather became an overseer in the sugarcane fields, one step above the Japanese laborers. Land was cheap, and he managed to buy one lot in Honolulu and another one to the north. The house in Honolulu still stands and is probably worth millions of dollars. The house my other great-grandfather built in California is probably worth millions of dollars too. Both men settled in places that became more desirable with each passing decade. I imagine both would be satisfied with such a fantastic outcome, but especially Grandpa Borges's father, who endured years of sacrifice and hardship as both a refugee and immigrant.

My grandfather's sisters kept track of me after my father, then my grandfather, and finally my grandmother passed away. So did my grandmother's sisters. I had a clan of elderly women, with names like Claire, Myrtle, and Queenie, who made me dresses, stuffed animals, and quilts. They sent me cards with cheerful-looking bears for my birthdays. Many of them were professional seamstresses and worked in large sewing shops. I learned to sew, crochet, and knit from them too. They never had idle hands at a get-together.

All of my grandfather's sisters who moved from Honolulu to the mainland to marry and raise families went back to Hawaii when they were widowed—and eventually, most of them were. No matter how their lives had been as wives, economically and emotionally, they all went home to live in the house where they had been born. This house had remained in the possession of the one maiden-great-aunt who had taken on the caretaking for my great-grandfather and grandmother, who lived into their late nineties. Getting old for these Hawaiian Portuguese meant going home, not to a "rest home" but to the family home. Everyone knew they would be cared for, and this security allowed them to be generous with me and with each other.

I remember my aunt Claire, a twin with such bad arthritis that she had to hold my hand when she walked downstairs. This made a big impact on me because I was only nine and couldn't imagine having "bad knees." She told me that when she went back to Honolulu, she was going to sit on the beach where the tide came in and let it wash over her. She said it was a cure for the pain she endured. Hawaiian people had their own ideas about how to get well and how to age. Aunt Margaret, the maiden aunt, also believed in the powers of love potions, evil spells, and medicine men called *kahunas.*

Married and divorced once, Margaret believed her ex-husband had slipped her a love potion, which had quickly worn off as soon as she married. "I never liked the man. Then suddenly I did. Then right away after I married him, I didn't like him again." She didn't believe in Western medicine at all, not even dentists. People considered her strange, even within her own family. But she fished in low tides and could husk a coconut with her bare hands until she was eighty and outlived all her brothers and sisters.

The first time I went to Hawaii was long after all but three of my grandfather's brothers and sisters had died. They had sold the big house and built a house on their land on the North Shore, near the Sacred Falls. The modern two-story house had a manicured garden that ended at the seawall. In the afternoons the tide would come up, and I would jump in and swim to the little bay a mile south. In the mornings I would sit outside and drink tea beside the koi pond and stare at the horizon, enjoying the gentle trade winds.

They were selling this beautiful house now because one sister and her husband wanted to move back to California to be near their children and grandchildren. Great-Aunt Margaret, the maiden aunt, and her sister Bea, who'd had a hard life with a mean, sick husband she had taken care of until his death, were moving into a smaller house in Honolulu. Margaret had sent for me so that I could spend a little time on the "family land" before it was sold.

There was a certain generosity in my grandfather's family that my grandmother's family lacked. The Hawaiian culture is forgiving. Life on the islands generated a different outlook than life in places like Ireland and Scotland. Before contact with the rest of the world in 1778, the Hawaiians had a well-run society based on cooperation and communal land use. After contact, only 10 percent of the population survived the germs and diseases that Captain Cook and his men carried. Hawaii before 1778 was as close to a Garden of Eden as any place on earth ever was or will be again. Even today, people in Hawaii feel happier than anywhere else in the United States in spite of widespread poverty. Living in so much natural beauty and spending time outside fosters the spirt of *aloha*, a potent word that evokes the way of life or spirit of the ancient Hawaiian culture.

When Great-Aunt Bea came "home," her advanced breast cancer in brief remission, Margaret, who had inherited the house and the money, took her sister on a trip around the world that lasted six months, with a long stop in Portugal. And again, it was Margaret who had thought of me before the family land was sold, though I had never set foot on Hawaii before. I guess they had a protocol. I later learned that before Captain Cook's inauspicious arrival, all land was shared and communal. Maybe Margaret, born and raised on Hawaiian soil, retained the essence of this old relationship to landownership. During our drive to the airport for my return home, we realized I had forgotten my lei. Margaret would not be talked out of driving back to get it. I missed my flight and had to spend six hours waiting for the next. In her mind it was a small price to pay. If I had forgotten my lei, the gods would have turned on me, and I never would have come back.

In my late twenties, I was working my way through graduate school as a single parent and had very little money. Getting a free ticket from Margaret had surprised me. The trip to Hawaii was my first experience of their rich, sensuous lives outside of the backyard luaus from my childhood in California. I wondered if my grandfather had missed this place. How fortunate he had been to grow up in Honolulu in the late nineteenth century. I don't think he ever went back with my grandmother. Maybe she would have been nicer, happier, if he had brought her home instead of living with her in her world. I think my grandmother would have grown contented, happy instead of dim. She might have respected my grandfather more and been less attached to her son. My father might have drawn closer to his father's ways and his people, less tied to his mother's need and disappointment.

My father's parents both came from big families, yet each had only one child. My father was spoiled, I think, and was dominated, just like his father, by my grandmother. Did my grandparents want more children? Or were they secretly relieved, having been traumatized by growing up with so many siblings? What kinds of relationships did husbands and wives have while raising ten or more children? My grandmother's family was an unhappy one. With ten daughters and no sons, my stern Protestant great-grandfather was outnumbered. My grandfather's family must have been happier, with an even mix of boys and girls. Honolulu back then had a high culture I can only imagine. People didn't have to work all the time to survive. The arts were part of daily life, and people were valued and rewarded for their creative efforts. The big house was near the Iolani Palace, after all. When my grandfather was born, Queen Liliuokalani still lived there. She was a benevolent ruler and had their respect and their devotion.

A talented musician and composer (best known for the popular song "Aloha Oe"), the queen spent her final days under house arrest. Locked in a room in her palace, she witnessed her beloved Hawaii swept away in a political grab that stole its sovereignty. During her reign, diplomats from all over the world had visited and danced and dined at her palace. The palace was airy, elegant, and very up-to-date, with indoor plumbing and electric lighting. It has stood the test of time. It was a place where people lived with grace and ease and beauty, not just a monument to power, like European palaces.

She and her husband were fine dancers too. Highly cultured people, they were known for their excellent food, intimate dinners, fine entertainment, and musical ability. The people in Hawaii value and cherish the sacred arts of dance, especially the hula. They identify themselves as singers, hula dancers, wood carvers, canoe makers, and genealogy experts, even when they have a doctorate from Harvard. What they value has to do with the spirit embedded in aloha, the joyful sharing of the energy of life, their traditions, and their skills.

Great-Aunt Margaret outlived her brothers and sisters. Great-Aunt Myrtle on my grandmother's side also outlived all her brothers and sisters. Both lived into their late nineties. Both of them took an interest in me until their deaths. They were the only ones, I guess, with the emotional space to see the bigger family pattern. I think the secret to a long life, or at least one of the secrets, is to live your own way— maybe even not have kids and a husband to worry about. Both Margaret and Myrtle were divorced and without children, which was unusual in that time. They were my favorites. The other women seemed disappointed and full of complaints, though they pitied their lonely "childless" sisters.

So although my father died when I was one, and I have felt more or less orphaned all my life, my Portuguese ancestors find me and guide me on my journey through flamenco. My first exposure to flamenco as a teenager and my return to it as an older women take me back to people who knew the importance of communal music-making, of the luau. When I dance flamenco, it feels right because it connects me to an invisible past that lives on through me. I feel close to lives that I can only intuit, like my father's.

A talented singer and piano player, my father became a sergeant in the army for eight years. He was a party man on the surface but a luau man under that. I'll bet he had never felt at home in the white mainland culture of the late 1940s or in his mother's stern Protestant family. He tried to compromise, becoming one of the first x-ray technicians and joining the army, but his heart was the heart of a musician. Women loved him too. He had Clark Gable looks and magnetism and loved the "high life." I can't imagine what my grandmother went through in losing her only son. She must have been seriously depressed. I think my grandfather was too, but he probably just got quieter, smoked more, and tried to stay out of my grandmother's way.

Their music was my inheritance. I have old records my father and grandfather recorded in the backyard, my grandfather playing one instrument or another, my father singing. I have the record with my father's favorite song, the one played at his funeral, Debussy's "Clair de Lune." How romantic he must have been. I believe I inherited that tendency because I love the feeling of time spent in the company of people who play instruments, sing, and dance. No wonder I am attracted to the flamenco studio, to a world that encourages collaborative, creative expression for people of all ages.

My mother's side of the family left nothing behind. They didn't build large homes for their families that still stand. They didn't own land. They didn't get together in their backyards and sing. They were better educated and more sophisticated than my father's family. My mother's father, Carl, was a Danish sea captain who spoke seven languages. Her mother, Anna, was an Austrian chef from Vienna. Unluckily, they arrived in the United States a decade too late, their fledgling fortunes dissolving in the Great Depression. Like salmon who couldn't find their way back upstream when their time came, they dwindled over time, unable to take root anywhere.

Flamenco is the song of migration. The people in southern Spain are from many cultures, oppressed, living in exile, suffering with dignity and grace. The real Gypsies are a mysterious people, tenacious and often hard-living. They brought with them to Spain's Andalusia influences from Africa, India, and Eastern Europe. The Polynesians have often been dominated and culturally stripped too. They too were travelers, navigating their way across the world on high seas in handmade canoes. They flounder without their traditions, their language, and their ceremonies.

While I was writing this chapter, one of my best friends died. After hearing she had taken a turn for the worse in the hospital, I went out to do errands and distract myself. Music seems the only natural response in such times. Like the Maori do when they mourn, I found myself singing. In my case, the song was Elton John's "Philadelphia Freedom." For no reason at all, this song came to me, though I had never really paid much attention to it before. I channeled the lyrics—"Shine a light through the eyes of the ones left behind. Shine a light. Shine a light. Won't you shine a light?" I later found out this was the time of her death.

I know when I go to flamenco class, I will dance with my grief. All the primary emotions have rooms in the house of flamenco. Flamenco gives me strength and the power to live with the immensity of life. I can lament and protest at the same time that I love. I experience a sense of homecoming even in the face of great loss. This is the heart of *duende*. This is the gift from my grandfather.

Chapter Nine
The Heart of Flamenco

My trips through Spain were quite adventurous
in the sense that, when I went there, what
influenced me was the people I met, the places
I ate, the *ambiente* all the way through.
—Teo Morca

I once heard a novelist compare plot to a clothesline. You
have to have someplace to hang the incidents of a story.
Often the reader hardly notices it, but it gives narrative co-
hesion. Flamenco became that for me, a running through-
line in my life that allowed the ordinary tangle of subplots
to find a home. I thought that at most, I'd dance until I
turned sixty. Maybe I would celebrate my birthday with a
trip to Spain and a week of classes in one of the studios in
Sevilla or Madrid. I researched a school in an Andalusian
town outside of Sevilla where I could live with a family,
study Spanish, and dance. Oh, happy thoughts!

Those first three years were like a rebirth. Each spring,
my dance friends and I looked forward to the June flamenco festival and the feast of live performances and intense workshops with the famous dancers from Spain. The
flurry of nine days spent sweating and studying in the studio and the nights in the theater became the highlight of

summer. I couldn't ask for more. Slowly, I moved from the beginner to the intermediate level. Classes became longer and more demanding. After three years, most of the people I had started with had disappeared, and I missed their fellowship. Some returned for brief intervals and then disappeared completely. A few stayed my friends outside of class.

My sixtieth birthday came and went. I was still at it, thoughts of stopping pushed into a hazy future. Though Spain seemed far away and less compelling than remaining in Albuquerque for the rush of the festival and the summer classes, I finally went to Spain in spring. It wasn't the trip I had imagined at sixty. I traveled with my husband and the desire to track flamenco, take field notes for this book, see some shows, and get a pair of handmade shoes at Don Flamenco's in Madrid. I was content to wander and soak up the *ambiente* that Teo Morca describes in his book *Becoming the Dance: Flamenco Spirit*. One of my friends, a flamenco dancer and painter, loaned me a biography on the famous bullfighter Manuel Benitez, or "El Cordobes." Though I had no interest in bullfighting, my friend told me it was a great way to learn about recent Spanish history. He was so right.

Or I'll Dress You in Mourning: The Story of El Cordobes and the New Spain He Stands For consumed me on the long flight over the Atlantic. The gripping story tells the life of a young Andalusian boy growing up under Franco's oppressive dictatorship. His father, a poor *campesino* involved in village politics, was imprisoned by Franco's forces. His mother struggled to raise Manuel and his five brothers and sisters in terrible poverty. Manuel faced every obstacle to become the legendary "El Cordobes." The moving account of this singular life provided a fascinating window into the Spanish culture of the twentieth century and helped me to understand in an intimate way the culture that produced flamenco.

The biographers, two skilled journalists, narrate the story with a rising line of tension that made it impossible to stop reading. I learned about the closed and often brutal society under Franco's reign, the feudal structure of the societies of southern Spain, and the history of raising and breeding bulls, all through the arc of one man's life. On the eve of his most historic bullfight, Manuel told his sister, who had loved him like a mother, "Don't cry, Angelita. Tonight, I'll buy you a house, or I'll dress you in mourning." He risked all, over and over, to become a hero for Spain's rural poor. He succeeded in spite of the harshest adversity.

I arrived in Spain curious about the intersecting paths of bullfighting and flamenco. I had no intention of watching a real fight. I still could not comprehend the killing of the bull or envision watching the process. Couldn't we keep everything on a symbolic level, please? I wanted to know more about the social forces behind this time-honored, highly ritualized sport. Bulls had appeared in my dreams at critical times in my life. I often found myself standing up to bulls that turned out to be curiously gentle. Flamenco dancers and bullfighters share the pose of taking a stand and facing the enormity of life with courage. The *bailaor* and the *torero* stand with feet planted on the earth, backs arched, chests lifted. Their heads are high, their gaze slightly over one shoulder. They are ready, poised and centered in enormous sacred power.

In the myths of the world, the bull figures prominently. For the ancient Greeks, bullfighting took the form of an actual bull leaping for them. Bulls figure in the symbolic and the aesthetic history of humankind dating back to prehistoric cave paintings. The sacrifice of the bull often was a sacred, ceremonial ritual. The bull represents nature's force and primal mysteries that human beings necessarily encounter. So though the bull is male, he is also, ironically, feminine as a representation of the natural world. And the gaudy bullfighter in his pink socks and tight pants also embraces a uniquely gendered ambivalence.

Anti-bullfighting sentiment in Spain and elsewhere reflects Spain's shift from an agrarian society to an industrial one. Northern Spain, richer and more urban, recently banned bullfighting. In Portugal the bull never dies in the ring but is slaughtered offstage at the end of the spectacle. As societies embrace technology and become removed from nature-based rhythms and the mythic element of "man" against nature, bullfighting has become less popular, more sanitized. Women have been bullfighters or have attempted to be. However, the idea of masculinity that is so encoded in the image of the matador denies most women the sex appeal that men have in the ring. A feminine man just is not the same as a masculine woman.

As an armchair Buddhist, I try to live a life that reflects my intentions to do no harm to myself or to others. This philosophy serves me well because I have an innate predisposition toward nonviolence. Why anyone watches a spectacle involving pain and suffering puzzles me at best and disgusts me at worst. Yet engagement with Spanish history and culture encourages a rethinking of some of my long-held preconceptions about good and bad and right and wrong. I must suspend judgment to experience the spirit of flamenco in its homeland.

I wonder if it might be better to celebrate the killing of the bull with pageantry and collective engagement than to repress it and have it spread into meaningless and random acts of violence common to today's society. Aren't our depressing, foul-smelling stockyards and our supermarket rows of meats wrapped in plastic and Styrofoam every bit as violent without the art and beauty and the community participation? Wasn't the absolute poverty that enveloped Spain before and during Franco's era a sustained form of violence? As an American who has grown up in a sanitized world, I have tried to avoid the truth about my participation in the unavoidable brutality that constitutes survival.

Ernest Hemingway and Garcia Lorca wrote about bullfights with deep respect and admiration. Why would the young, starving peasant Manuel Benitez spend his whole life working toward the single goal of becoming a bullfighter? What was it that I couldn't see or appreciate and that, in fact, I dismissed as irrelevant because I considered the practice barbaric? Perhaps the public enactment of an ancient ritual, a fight between human beings and nature, allowed brutality not to fester beneath the surface and manifest in individual or collective psychosis. This path through flamenco urges me not to look away.

As I witness the decline of my own country, cruelty is everywhere. I see it in the inhumane treatment of people who are denied health care and shelter. In any city center, I see walking refugees with their carts or their stained backpacks, many released from jails and prisons with no earthly place to go. Human beings sleep on the sidewalks, worse off than the dogs the upper middle class dote on for comfort. Hatred and meanness seep into domestic and global political discourse, the media, and the movies. It seems we want to blame, reject, and punish more than we want to understand, assist, and include. The news narrates the spectacle of madmen with guns and knives who with the least provocation kill anyone in their path. How does a culture contain violence and purge it through artistic expression and ritualized ceremonies so that a society can function without falling into chaos?

Perhaps ritualized violence keeps random violence in check, allowing people to vent their natural anger in socially controlled forums. Aristotle coined the term *catharsis*, where through a vicarious dramatic experience, an audience is "purged of excessive emotions." When people watch a play, listen to a symphony, or attend a bullfight or a football game, something is released, allowing for a new balance. As the plane landed in Madrid, I jotted many questions in my notebook and highlighted the sections on *tablaos* and bullrings in my travel guides.

During our four days in Madrid, we saw two flamenco shows. The first show was on the top of my list of things to do. Café Chinitas, a prominent venue for the flamenco renaissance of the 1960s, was walking distance from our hotel. I booked tickets from our hotel with anticipation. On our way that night to the café, we passed an ornate Catholic church and went inside to have a look. A priest was giving evening mass, but only two people, a young man and an older woman, were there to participate. I couldn't help but wonder what would happen if no one came at all. As day turned to night, I experienced the overpowering fatigue and vague sense of foreboding that come with jet lag. What if my romantic nature had led me down another blind alley?

A lackluster performance by no-longer-young artists before a small crowd of wealthy diners disappointed me. The show lacked *duende* and left me feeling discouraged. Was I searching for a relic from the past? Had flamenco in Spain run its course and become just another form of commercial entertainment? I was grateful that my husband, though he agreed the show seemed rather tired, enjoyed himself. He'd had no expectations, and just being in a café in Madrid on our first night in Spain satisfied him.

The next day, somewhat chastened, I searched for an illustrious bullfighter's bar, Torro del Oro. My husband, used to my squeamishness around violence, seemed shocked that I wanted to visit a bar full of stuffed bull heads. I called it a literary exploration. Rumor had it that Hemingway had drunk there in the hot afternoons. Madrid has several large plazas throughout the city. Plaza Mayor, perhaps the most famous of them of all, was lined with shops and cafés. Following the guidebook, we soon stumbled on the hundred-year-old bar, a living shrine to the history of bullfighting.

I timed our arrival after lunch and before dinner, in the quiet hour when waiters put out fresh linens and place settings. When approached, I nodded and smiled, declining firmly but politely to be seated. In reviews of the bar, people commented that the waiters had hustled them to buy expensive drinks and food. I glanced around with awe. The heads of notorious black bulls killed in the ring by prominent matadors hung like paintings between photographs of matadors in their "suits of lights." Each matador was being stomped, gored, tossed, or treated for a variety of wounds. The waiters quietly followed me with their eyes, pausing from their work.

My journey ended at a golden shrine. In the gilded case hung a "suit of lights"—a jacket heavy with gold and silver embroidery—a sword, a black hat with two peaks, and other relics from El Cordobes's historic 1967 fight. With Franco, the Spanish dictator, in attendance and two-thirds of the country watching him on television, Manuel had fought too long and lost, suffering a severe injury from his half-blind nemesis, Impulsivo. Though he recovered and went on to fight for another period, he never recaptured the magical heights that had led him to that day.

On the wall to the right of the shrine was a photograph of Julio Aparicio, a contemporary bullfighter, at the moment he was gored. The horn of the huge bull Opiparo pierced the back of Julio's throat and came out his open mouth like a tongue. Man and beast locked into a grizzly position. I later learned Julio had survived! My husband, too, stood in awe. When we left, the waiters looked up, met my eyes, and seemed to approve of my visit. I savored the respect I experienced then and off and on in my two weeks in Spain. However, when I lost my way, I met with impatience and disapproval that taught me to be prepared about where I was going or what I wanted to do.

Spain absorbed my thoughts and my imagination. The dark and the light mingled like twin rivers in the moonlight to produce glints of sparkling insight. I had the address of a small shoemaker's shop on one of the cobblestone streets of the old city. Don Flamenco's storefront was modest and unmarked. Only the beautifully handcrafted flamenco shoes in the little window revealed the shop's identity. If I hadn't known to look, I might have walked right past. When we entered, the handsome, bearded shoemaker stood behind a small counter with several shelves of shoes behind him. The shop reminded me of the shoe repair shops I had grown up with in North Beach, San Francisco. There would always be a man, usually quite elderly, sitting humbly at his work, rows of repaired shoes on crude shelves lining the walls.

This shoemaker spoke no English, but he soon fitted me for a pair of two-tone dove-gray suede shoes made to the specific dimensions of my feet. To be served by the shoemaker himself! To pick the colors and the height and width of the heels and be sized correctly! What good fortune! If you haven't seen a pair of handmade flamenco shoes, you have missed a work of art. Paying cash, I hoped my shoes would arrive in the six weeks Don Flamenco sincerely promised. They did, but if they hadn't, I still would have considered the money well spent.

We asked around and discovered that the best *tablaos* were at a restaurant bar called Café Patos. After following Rick Steve's advice about saving money and avoiding the dinner part of the show at Café Chinitas, I decided to splurge on this dinner and show. I didn't want to sit and watch other people eat fabulous food while I drank sangria and staved off hunger with dry bread. If the show disappointed, at least I would have dined well.

The venue, however, was completely different from the previous one. People ate in a classic European, old-fashioned dining room with a long, elegant bar and polished mirrors. Small round tables with crisp white table linens took up the rest of the floor space. Waiters with starched white aprons and black ties served us wonderful meals of roasted chicken with sprigs of rosemary, new potatoes and garden vegetables, wine, and fresh loaves of bread. Then we were herded into a small room, perched shoulder to shoulder on flimsy wooden chairs.

Waiting for the show to begin, I had a sinking feeling that this would be another tourist trap. I didn't like how they had packed us into the room and hustled drinks before the show. My worries vanished the moment the musicians and the dancers stepped onto the stage. A rising "Olé!" erupted from the crowd, followed by a reverent silence. The troupe took their seats on old wooden chairs, shifting to get comfortable, centering their minds and their hearts, entering that invisible interior space where their music would begin. The male singers were young and bold, the guitarist had a quiet power as he cradled his instrument, and the dancers, a man and a woman, were subdued in a way that told me they had a lot to give.

Time stood still from the moment they entered the stage until the show was over, almost two hours later. It was as if I inhaled, and then two hours later I exhaled. We had done it! We had experienced the power and the joy of *duende*. Everyone knew it. Our bodies and minds were singing. I wanted to wait an hour and take in the midnight show. It had all gone too fast, and now it was over? I wanted to stay and be part of it again, perhaps have more distance so I could appreciate the artistry of the lead dancers. I had fallen into a trance. I was in love with Spain. The years on the dance floor in Albuquerque had brought me to this un-repeatable night in Madrid. "Olé!" We clapped and clapped and shouted. "Olé! Olé!" We leapt to our feet, our faces shining with pleasure, and clapped some more.

As I traveled south through Granada on our way to-ward Sevilla, the overlapping passions of the bullfighting and flamenco worlds guided my way. We made a special trip to Ronda, a small Andalusian village, to see its famous bullring. Hemingway dedicated "Fiesta" and *Death in the Afternoon* to bullfighters from this town. The bullring, per-haps Spain's oldest, dates back to the sixteenth century. We wandered the places where the bulls were sequestered and down the narrow dark tunnels leading into the ring. Unlike stockyards or even barns, the stalls were fresh and clean, without acrid livestock smells.

Standing in the hot sun in the center of the immac-ulately swept bullring, I searched the stands. I imagined the bull breaking out of the long dark tunnel and into the blazing light, stunned by the roaring crowds and the luring picadors. I imagined the poor bull, disoriented, homesick, and thoroughly enraged, entering the ring. I imagined the matador, his heart racing, his mind acute, prepared to face the bull to the death. The energy flows from the people in the stands and beats in the heart of the bull and the mata-dor. Time opens into infinity. Everyone roars.

I searched the level, sandy ground for evidence of centuries of bloodshed. The cleanly swept earth bore no trace. Though still an active bullring for part of the year, it was as pristine as a cloister and resembled one too, with its arches and columns. I noticed the wooden gates with fading stencils of the heads of bulls wreathed in garlands. A small art gallery near the entrance included a Picasso. In bold economic strokes, the painter captured the absolute *duende* of the moment when the bull dances close to the matador and the red cape flows between them like a wave.

I had booked our hotel in Sevilla from Madrid. The week after Semana Santa, which culminates in Easter, room rates were at the lowest they would be for the year. I couldn't quite believe our luck! We were going to stay at a gorgeous old hotel in a restored former palace with a rooftop patio overlooking the enormous, gothic Sevilla Cathedral. Just a few blocks in the other direction was La Maestranza de Sevilla, the most renowned bullring in Spain.

The flamboyant bullring and cathedral were built to boldly display Spain's wealth. The cathedral, built on the site of a mosque, dated back to the 1100s. Having taken more than four centuries to complete, it supposedly houses Christopher Columbus's tomb. It is said that the parishioners who financed it, not without considerable sacrifice, wanted people who came afterward to see the cathedral and think they were madmen. The altar in the main chapel had taken one master craftsman his entire lifetime to complete. What dedication, what excess, and what folly! Earthquakes over the centuries collapsed the main dome, and everything had to be rebuilt several times. No matter, these madmen continued to build, obsessed with their singular mission.

The bullring too took over a hundred years to finish and reflected the styles of generations of architects. We were going to spend five nights in this setting. It took a bit of enchantment to dream big. Sevilla arrived in my life like a beautiful haughty woman and an aloof handsome man. People's voices carried the edges of song, of argument, and of lament. Emotions welled up and spilled out into art, into tears, into lovemaking.

I sat in the hotel's walled garden and ordered a big bottle of *aqua con gas*. A man broke into song at the corner table. Hustling tickets for a show that evening, he enticed us with his plaintive voice. The day's bullfight was being televised in the bar. The courtyard had two fountains and lush plants. I savored the cool shadows, the plush sound of running water, the rich Sevillan voices, and this welcome respite from the relentless afternoon heat. No American tourists here—just upwardly mobile Spaniards, many of them bullfighting *aficionados*. I later discovered that this was where the bullfighters and their retinues stayed as well. The bullfighters returning after a fight, dressed in their flashy ceremonial outfits, remains an image I will never forget.

A hush came over the lobby as the matador and his retinue entered the hotel like nobility entering a court. I had just walked in from the cool, shady courtyard, and their appearance sharpened my lulled senses. Had they just been in a fight to the death? Except for a little dust on their cloth shoes, they were immaculate. They sauntered up to the front desk. The dashing matador captivated our attention. His golden embroidered jacket, his peaked black cap, and his tight knee-length pants, embroidered up the sides like the jacket, signified his prestige. His pants gave way to hot-pink stockings and black flats with little bows. I mean, really!

The picador, another gorgeous man with classic features, stood to one side. Wearing armor on his right leg and foot, which I learned protected his horse when he taunted the bull, he walked a little more slowly than the others, the chain making a distinct clanking sound on the polished tile floors. The *banderilleros* or "peons," decorated in silver embroidery, had an easy, familiar way, joking and smiling with each other. They loved our attention, and we loved giving it to them. Keys in hand, the matador and his companions went to a special elevator leading to a private wing with private suites to celebrate. We all turned to one another with wide eyes. We had seen royalty.

Sevilla is not for wimps. No one pampered me there. Yet a string of magical moments punctuated my days. If you were up and running and knew where you were headed, all was well. But if you were lost or indecisive, forget it. The shaded courtyard became a place of refuge where I regained my composure in the hot afternoons. At my flamenco school in the States, the teachers expected us to muscle on, to toughen up, to endure the suffering that came with fatigue, heat, muscle aches, and general difficulty. They were as hard on themselves as they were on their students. It was that edge that I recognized in Sevilla.

Every glint of light had a corresponding element of shadow. Every song carried a potential for love or anger, often both.

I planned our last day in Sevilla with care. I would walk to the flamenco museum. I would haunt the many flamenco stores brimming with hand-embroidered shawls, painted fans, rhinestone mantillas, and ruffled skirts and dresses in every fabric imaginable. I had fallen into the heart of flamenco. Before the sun set, though, we would walk a few blocks to the cathedral and stroll the wide cobblestone promenades. We would hear flamenco guitar wafting through the cool currents of the evening air like the scent of Sevilla's famous orange blossoms. Flying buttresses, bell towers, and the great domes inspired dreams that bridge centuries of desire for transcendence. Our hearts would resonate and sing out with response. Olé. Life is brief. Life is sweet. Olé.

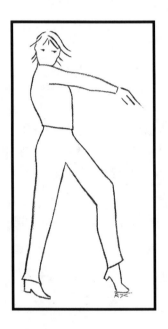

Chapter Ten

Courageous Action

Better to die than live mechanically a life
that is a repetition of repetitions.
—D. H. Lawrence, *Women in Love*

Stories about people who decide to live from their deepest intentions inspire me. Often their call to action comes as a stark message from fate. Something happens that wakes them up and irrevocably alters their life. It could be a death, financial ruin, a divorce, or an accident. Life certainly gives us many opportunities to try something different rather than repeat the same patterns that have brought us to the present. These stories hold the spirit of *duende*. The protagonists respond to life's challenges with an intention that transforms their lives, launching them into a destiny they had never imagined awaited.

Joseph Campbell came to his theory of the hero's journey after an unexpected period of relative poverty and isolation. Born and raised in wealth, he was attending Columbia with the financial support of his family when he suddenly found his studies disrupted during the Great Depression. His father could no longer pay for his education. Campbell, forced to drop out of college, read for the next five years, earning a modest sum reviewing books for several publishing houses. He lived quietly and inexpensively in a small cabin in the woods.

Studying on his own, he often read up to nine hours a day. When his father's fortunes returned, Campbell had discovered his life's work. He finished his master's at Columbia in medieval literature but dropped out of further studies when his unique interdisciplinary approach to a doctorate lacked faculty support. Teaching at Sarah Lawrence College, he wrote many articles and books, such as *The Hero with a Thousand Faces*. If he had never been forced to quit his studies or if he had squandered the opportunity to study independently, he might not have made his singular contribution to scholarship. He might have become a distinguished professor, but his cross-cultural thinking on myths and symbols never would have had time to incubate and come into being.

Sister Antonia's life and work provide another story of transformation. When I read *Prison Angel*, the story of a former Beverly Hills housewife who, after a divorce and raising seven children, decided to go live and work in La Mesa Penitentiary in Tijuana, I could hardly believe it. Sister Antonia defied the rules of her church that prevented her from becoming a nun as a divorced woman. She sold her belongings, sewed her own habit, and showed up on the steps of the prison. People must have questioned her sanity.

Having been inside California's prisons to visit my son on his heartbreaking descent into mental illness, I have witnessed the endless suffering experienced by both the prisoners and their families. I have seen mothers fall apart after visiting their sons. Screaming and sobbing, they were forcefully removed by guards from the waiting room. I have watched a mother age decades in just a few years. She drove ten hours each way to visit her son on weekends. Her son was serving forty years for a botched home invasion in his early twenties that had given him "three strikes," and he had no hope of parole. Sentenced at twenty-one in Orange County, the month after the three-strikes law went into effect, he had gotten one strike for stealing a screwdriver, another for breaking and entering, and the final for stealing a VCR. Forty years and a family broken. I know the helpless feeling of witnessing something that is terribly wrong and not being able to change it. We all do.

Imagine living in a cell in a Mexican prison with worse conditions than many prisons in the United States. Imagine serving those in need and living with them, instead of ministering to them from a safe, bureaucratic distance. Sister Antonia's willingness to suffer with the prisoners in the same conditions transformed the prisoners' images of themselves as outcasts. "Something happened to me when I saw men behind bars. When I left, I thought a lot about the men. When it was cold, I wondered if the men were warm; when it was raining, if they had shelter," she told the *Times* in a 1982 interview. "I wondered if they had medicine and how their families were doing. You know, when I returned to the prison to live, I felt as if I'd come home." Thirty years later, she not only had been recognized as a "real" nun by the Catholic Church but also had formed her own order for "mature women." The Eudist Servants of the Eleventh Hour allowed women who were past their childbearing years to join with Sister Antonia to work with and for the

most underrepresented people in society—because not to
do it, for them, would be a life half-lived.

Then there is John Francis. He responded to an oil spill
in the San Francisco Bay in the 1970s with the decision
not to use any transportation that relied on fossil fuel. He
basically walked everywhere for the next twenty-two years.
And after the first five years, because he kept getting into
arguments with people over his radical position, he decided
to stop talking too. Miraculously, he finished his PhD and
wrote the book *Planet Walker*, the account of his decision
and his journey.

When asked why he did what he did, he answered
that he had wanted to "do something" but hadn't known
what to do. The senseless environmental disaster in the
San Francisco Bay that he loved had triggered his decision.
He practiced what he believed and lived with the consequences. Surprisingly, those consequences now include a
job with the US Coast Guard to help manage oil spills.
Along the way, he gave up smoking, took up the banjo, and
taught himself to paint with watercolors.

Another inspiration is Jimmy Baca, a once-illiterate
former gang member from New Mexico. He learned to read
and write when he was twenty-two while serving time in
prison. In *A Place to Stand*, he describes his life and his unexpected discovery of words, of the power of language, and
his own awakening to a world he hadn't realized existed.
Not only did he become literate, but he read and educated
himself to become a poet, writer, and prison activist. He
wrote and acted in the movie *Blood In Blood Out* about
prison gangs. His passion for language opened the door to

a world filled not only with pain and suffering but also with hope and connection. For him, the moment of *duende* came when he could read simple words and string them together in a simple unit of meaning: a sentence.

Orphaned at a young age, after which he lived with his grandmother and then on the streets, Jimmy Baca went to prison for six years, spending half that time in solitary confinement. What should have broken his spirit liberated him. After learning how to read and write, he used his newly discovered literacy to craft poems. He left prison, transformed from a criminal into what he calls "a poet to the people." His desire to speak to and for the disenfranchised saved his life. It gave him, in his own words, "a place to stand."

In her memoir *To Dance on Sands*, Marta Becket tells the story of her life in the middle of the Mojave Desert. She was a New York ballerina traveling across the United States with her husband when her car broke down in the Mojave Desert. Stranded in a forsaken town in Amargosa, Marta found an abandoned opera house. She decided then and there to stay and renovate the building into a theater. It was a shocking thing to do, and her fellow dancers in New York thought she had lost her mind. She spent several years painting extensive murals of her ideal sixteenth-century audience on the wall. Balconies overflowed with men and women in their finery and costumes. They flirted and laughed. Each day at five o'clock, she performed for her imaginary audience. Slowly but surely, real audiences came.

Though her husband left her, she went on to thrive and to dance for another forty years. She also attracted another

man, who became her life-long companion and dance part-
ner. Dancing into her late eighties, she dedicated her life
to her creative process and to saving the wild horses of the
desert, who were being corralled, captured, and threatened
with extinction. Marta created a life that was exciting, productive, and uniquely her own. In the process she became
an advocate for the spirit of creativity that needs to run
free, like her beloved horses.

When I taught at Humboldt State, I included Julia
Butterfly Hill's memoir in my Women and Nature course.
An almost near-death experience in an auto accident pro-
pelled Julia into a search for meaning. She ended up living
in a redwood tree, Luna, for two years to protest the logging
of the old-growth forests. She writes, "I had no clue what
I would do, but I knew I was meant to do something." In
The Legacy of Luna, she describes her metamorphosis into
a famous "tree-sitter." Though it is a story about saving the
redwoods and Julia's special connection to the giant tree
Luna, it is also a story of standing up for something without
equivocation. These stories have passion, conviction, and
resistance embedded in them.

Retirement these days has become a tricky issue.
People claim to want to work into their seventies and
eighties and stay productive. Often, underlying this claim
is the simple fact that people haven't saved enough to stop
working. My generation, the baby boomers, also engage in
illusions of immortality. Yet retirement can be a time when,
if health and financial matters permit, a person can travel,
develop new skills, or just daydream. I know that men, historically, have not done too well in their retirements, their

masculinity enmeshed in their ability to go out there and earn a living. I expect that now that women have entered the workforce, they will have the same problems adjusting to the emptiness of freedom.

Phillip Moffitt shares his story of retiring in his forties, selling *Esquire* magazine and setting out on an uncertain spiritual path with the intention of setting no goals. He found his life had been a series of goals that he had set and met for himself. Each time he met a goal, it left him feeling unsettled and empty. He wanted to live without a goal and to turn inward and focus on spiritual development. In *Dancing with Life*, he shares his experience of leaving the marketplace to become a Buddhist teacher at Spirit Rock Meditation Center. Retirement allowed him to become more and do more than he could have imagined. He had to stop and trust his intuition. Having the money to retire at forty was a huge factor in his journey, but many people with wealth continue their business lives because they like the rush of earning money and the identity that work provides, even if it leaves them feeling empty at the end of the day.

In Carolyn Heilbrun's book *The Last Gift of Time: Life beyond Sixty*, she explores the many freedoms that aging brings for women if they are smart enough to realize them. Oh darn, men don't follow you down the street in cars, whistling. Oh darn, your children don't call. Oh darn, your husband is preoccupied with his own crisis of aging. Finally—yes, finally—a woman can take off the corset of femininity she has worn since adolescence and do whatever it is she wants to do without notice. Heilbrun compares women's aging to King Lear's, but with favorable results.

When Lear gives it all away, he has nothing. Women, how-ever, have been carrying the baggage for men, so when they let it go, there is literally "the last gift of time."

As a scholar and women's studies professor, I have been mindful of the relationship between economics and free-dom. This certainly isn't absolute, but it is often the case that women end up with less money and fewer options in their final years. Also, our society portrays older men as sexy but women as less so. Heilbrun, a white educated woman with enough money to do as she pleased, enjoyed her last gift of time tracking persistent desires that had in-cubated for a lifetime. Why, she asks, should she squander such rare freedom for women?

In her 1931 novel *All Passions Spent*, Vita Sackville-West tells the story of an elderly widow who has devoted her life to her husband and her children. For decades, she lived the life of a diplomat's wife and mother. In her older years, the children expect her to become their burden since she no longer has a function. She surprises everyone with a plan of her own. She goes to live in a house she fell in love with before she married and lives her remaining years in a place of her own choice. She follows the buried narrative of her inner life. She forms new relationships and finds herself quite content. Her family can't fathom this unexpected renaissance in their aged mother.

Duende, an act of resistance. This is the moment when you tell your children you are not going to live with them. No, thank you very much! I plan to buy my own house, the house I fell in love with forty years ago. It is the moment in solitary confinement when you string together letters of the alphabet into a word and fall in love with language. Or you stop driving in cars and discover the wonders of walking and listening. Or you sleep in a tree for two years. Or you live in the middle of the Mojave Desert and dance to an audience you painted on the walls until a live audience finds you. Or you decide to become a nun even though you are divorced, and you sew your own habit.

On a more modest level, dancing flamenco is my act of resistance. I resist sitting in a chair, watching my life acted out by others. I resist letting my body slip away. I resist a culture of secondhand emotions and secondhand experiences. I am saving my own life. I am preparing to stand up to fight for social justice in unexpectedly personal ways. Dancing flamenco keeps me strong, head up, back straight. I can look life in the eyes.

Some people refer to this kind of engagement as a calling. It is also a protest. You find out you just can't do what you were doing before. And you have to do something, so off you go. The women's movement of the sixties and seventies embraced the slogan "The personal is political." I have always believed that lasting change occurs at this personal level. For some people this takes the form of collective political action, and for others it takes the form of a new way of life. No two people respond to their calling in the same way. *Duende* is authentic and impossible to reproduce. As with all true homecomings, *duende* is a deeply personal and irrefutable experience. Let's just say you have no doubt about it when it happens.

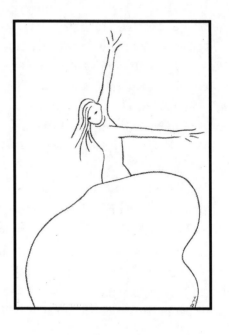

Chapter Eleven
On the Last Day

Everywhere else ... death comes, and they
draw the curtains. Not in Spain.
—Garcia Lorca

Death takes its own time. Or should I say, death has its own time. When my dear friend died, it shocked us. Her decline took three weeks from start to finish. Of course, she must have had premonitions, but she kept those secret, maybe even from herself. I admit I carried around a sense of foreboding that no one else seemed to share. I sensed her leaving like the ebbing tide, pulling back into the great depths of the soul of the ocean. Nothing seemed to abate her journey out once it started. Stents put into her veins the week before or her being in a heart hospital when her heart stopped were like a bulletproof vest made of cardboard. What went wrong? People's hearts just don't stop and stay stopped anymore. People get bypasses, stents, and pacemakers. They even get another heart!

The elderly now live into their nineties, some with quality of life and many without. And quality of life includes financial and emotional well-being. The wonders of modern medicine shout that death is shameful, like selling stocks too short or, god forbid, paying capital gains. So dying a few weeks short of her seventy-second birthday, my friend died too young. I'm not sure she would have enjoyed another decade and possibly another after that. Until she was hospitalized, she had been working full-time, living a richly engaged and independent life.

But increasing physical limitations had haunted her through her late sixties. Her knees had been replaced, and her weight, which had plagued her most of her life, remained an issue. She was professionally and personally connected to her life. On the day she died, she had a trip planned to visit me and another friend in New Mexico for a long weekend in Taos. Her calendar was full six months into the future. She didn't want to die. But she also didn't want to be dependent or disabled or give up her long and successful career as a Jungian analyst.

She probably would have grown to accept arthritic pain and increasing limits on her mobility. A realist who treasured spending time with her three grandchildren, she might have joked and smiled and carried on despite knowing that she was, in fact, disabled. That would not, however, have been her preference. So her death had a certain *duende* to it, a certain passion that deaths from long illnesses or after a long life never have. Elizabeth's heart stopped shortly after breakfast while a good friend sat beside her. She was about to be transferred to a rehab facility in a few days, and no one expected this would be her last morning. I can picture her smiling and joking with her friend, being her jovial self, right up to the cardiac event. She lingered between worlds on life support until her family arrived to weep loving tears as she was released.

The bull got her. I can see him—black as midnight, so black his coat shines cobalt-blue in the hot August sun. His horns crest around his head like two new moons. He has come for her. Nature's force saturates his enormous, liquid brown eyes. Is this love? Anger? Perhaps joy? What do they see in one another's eyes as they confront each other at the edge between worlds? One thing is certain: Elizabeth stands bold and bright in her suit of lights that glint and sparkle in the sun. The crowds cheer madly from the stands, a thousand hands clapping like thunder. The shadowless light of noon jumps and dazzles the bull, dazzles the light, dazzles the audience. Woman and beast square off, feet planted firmly on the cleanly swept dry earth. The crowd roars in unison, "Olé, olé!" as my friend gathers her red cape like a fiery dragon around her stout body.

"Suit of lights," *el traje de luces*, is a perfect name for the costume matadors wear into the bullring. One myth has it that Goya, the eighteenth-century Spanish painter, designed it. A highly ritualized costume, it ensures maximum visibility, a bright flame in the brightest light. The stiff jacket, with its sequins and embroidered golden threads, the tight pants like aristocrats wore in the courts of old, and the hot-pink socks and small red cape set the matador apart from his assistants. He is accompanied in this *corrida de torros*, or running of the bulls, by his entourage, the highest-ranking wearing suits of silver, *trajes de plata*. The assistants adhere to strict protocol. On horseback they engage the bull. Only the matador reigns supreme, a sun king. Only he has the honor of killing the bull when death arrives. He stands with dignity and courage, alone and on foot, in this final, public act.

Life expectancy is a fluid thing. Two hundred years ago in the United States, life expectancy was twenty-four. One hundred years ago, it was forty-eight. Now it is seventy-eight and climbing. So I'll use the number seventy-eight. Everyone wants to live to eighty or ninety, but the odds are you are doing better than average if you reach eighty. With this calculation, my friend fell short by seven years. But in the context of human history, she lived longer than 99 percent of the people who ever walked the planet. She didn't spend her accumulated assets, material and psychological, on long-term care and endless medical procedures. She didn't have to eat like an old lady or live like one, measured and prudent. She didn't have to put away her suit of lights for a chenille robe and watch reruns of her past performances in her mind, hell on earth for a true extrovert.

We have redefined the word "old." So maybe she could have lived longer. But not the way she wanted to live, working full-time, driving the Los Angeles freeways in the fast lane in her little hybrid car, eating good food, drinking wine, and throwing intimate dinner parties. She lived large, like the Leo personality she was. She "got out," the phrase she used for death in her last years, before she was taken to task for her sins. If she had lived as a disabled and aging woman, she would have had to submit to collective judgments. Never lost the forty pounds: one point down. Never faced the fact of that extra glass of wine: one point down. Didn't get enough exercise: another point down. The list would have grown as her doctor's appointments and medications increased. Her conversations would have become the usual conversations of the "elderly," circling around topics like pacemakers, blood pressure, arthritis, and cholesterol. In her own words, "Not a pretty picture."

While she was in the hospital for her first rounds of tests, I was studying the *segudillas* with a teacher from Spain. Another annual Flamenco Festival's classes and night performances had brought dancers and students together from all over the world. The slow-building intensity of the *segudillas* never fails to capture me. This dance begins like a dirge, with the somber power of lament. As with the opening of Beethoven's "Moonlight" sonata or Debussy's "Clair de Lune," I hear the first few chords, and no matter what I am thinking, feeling, or doing, the mood of the music takes me to another dimension, where birth and death and love and loss all swirl in the depths of my heart. I am lifted, magically, to the borders where all things end and begin. My breath deepens as I surrender to the music.

We all go a little mad during the festival. Intoxicated by the flood of classes and performances, we fall in love with the music and our teachers. We fall in love with life. The *ambience* of the flamenco world imported directly from Spain carries us to unexpected heights. We stay out late and take demanding classes in the impossibly hot afternoons. The teacher we watched performing in the theater the night before gives us instruction. We remember her passion and skill as she stands before us, a bank of dusty mirrors behind her, and feel that this is the real thing.

Right now! This moment! There is no place else in the world we want to be. Young and old, we all feel the intoxication. The guitar player who lingered at the door, smoking a cigarette with a faraway look in his sleepy eyes, now sits in a corner, draped over his guitar, picking up the cues from our teacher with renewed respect, because he too saw her performance and knows she is among the great. Truly and simply great.

There is a big fire going on this year. In addition to the intense June heat, suffocating smoke clogs the air. It feels like the apocalypse. I remember some years back seeing a movie about a village under a volcano. Just like in Pompeii, everyone in the village lives as if death is not possible the next minute. The mother of one of the main characters is the talk of the town. A recent widow, she has taken up ice skating on a small pond in one of the parks. She loves wearing her ice-skating outfit and taking lessons from her handsome, much younger teacher. All she wants to do, it seems, is ice-skate. Her son is worried about what people think. No one is having much fun or minding their own business except the old woman on the ice. And when the volcano erupts and everyone dies, she's in the middle of a pirouette, a smile on her face.

Our guitarist starts to play, and our teacher begins the class. The world outside this dark, dusty dance studio vanishes. The stunning male dancer we saw on opening night shows up in the doorway. He wears baggy sweatpants and a pink T-shirt, his blond hair pulled back in a ponytail. Our teacher demonstrates a pattern we learned the day before and instructs us to repeat it. Then she runs to the door for a passionate kiss. The pulse of the room quickens. How romantic they are! How in love! Young and old, the women on the dance floor want to be her. The men are inspired to love and be brave, accomplished, and adored. What more could anyone ever ask for?

Garcia Lorca, the poet who fostered the flamenco renaissance in 1930s Spain, was murdered three days before the outbreak of the Spanish Civil War by the anticommunist death squads. They shot him and threw him into an unmarked grave. By some accounts, he was forced to dig his own grave first. Though he was not political in the usual sense, his open homosexuality and his writing doomed him as the fascists gained control of Spain. He lived his short time on earth with the spirit of *duende*, facing and speaking out against oppression in his beloved Spain.

In his essay "Theory and Play of *Duende*," Lorca contrasts *duende* with the artist's muse or the contemplative's angels. Lorca writes that "with *duende* it is easier to love, to understand, and be certain of being loved and understood." *Duende* heals the opposites, brings life and death into the ring, ignites the passion that makes the journey between life and death something more than just a mechanical, repeatable pattern.

I danced while my friend was dying. I danced as my son went back to prison. Much later, I danced when unexpectedly he died, deprived of medical care in a "sobering cell" at four o'clock in the afternoon. I danced as my sister was diagnosed with lung cancer and recovered. I danced through economic panic and natural disasters. I have danced the good times too, through my daughter's college graduation and professional triumphs and at weddings (my own included) and birthday celebrations. I have danced my way through time, with time, in spite of time.

Flamenco is the sacred fire that accepts all offerings. When I went to the flamenco museum in Sevilla, the mixed-media history of flamenco included dances that demonstrated the whole range of emotions and experiences: love, sex, death, joy, anger, and revolt. One quote I jotted in my journal that day was that "flamenco is a protest to no one." Each person must and can stand up with her own unique destiny.

On my last day in Sevilla, I returned to the flamenco museum while my husband explored the city. A little early for the afternoon show, I sat in the empty theater in front of the empty stage, my notebook on my lap and pen in hand. The skylight overhead dramatically backlit a single chair and a large tree branch suspended by ropes twenty feet over my head. To my left, through the open doors of the dance studio, a teacher counted the rhythm of a *palo*: "One, two, *three*, four, five, *six*, seven, *eight*, nine, *ten*, eleven, *twelve*."

With his back to an attentive group of women, the instructor demonstrated the footwork with precise, effortless steps. Then he faced the class to watch them repeat his footwork with the correct syncopation. A handsome, lithe *gitano* with dark hair slicked back, he wore on his finely featured face the temperamental expression that many male flamenco dancers have and that most women find incredibly sexy.

A dancer in the back row caught my eye. She looked more like a New Jersey housewife—or my image of one—than a flamenco dancer. Her bobbed gray hair and short plump body contrasted with her long, red ruffled skirt, black top and shoes, and sparkling silver earrings. Yet in every way she belonged. Her movements were sure and expressive, and her pale face glowed with an inner joy that I understood, happiness a cloud under her feet.

Watching her, the writer in me created a backstory for her life. Maybe she was a retired grammar school teacher or a librarian. A recent widow perhaps. Or maybe her doctor or lawyer husband had suddenly off and left her for a younger woman. She had decided to take a flamenco class at the local community college at the advice of her therapist. And here she was, dressed in her flowing skirt and flamenco shoes, living a life as rich and lyrical as the poetry she had written in her private diary at fourteen. I could watch her dance for hours.

Satisfied with the students' performance, the teacher asked them to stop and then repeated the sequence. This time he sang the words to the *palo.* Backs became more erect, chins lifted, and shoulders moved up and back as students deepened into their movements. I shut my eyes and savored song and sound as thirty pairs of shoes drummed the patterns of the dance on the wooden floor. I realized I was not a tourist or even an observer. I was part of this flamenco world through my own study and practice.

I opened my journal and wrote for a while until a rather disheveled-looking man reeking of cigarettes sat down on the chair beside me and said in easy Spanish, "You dance flamenco? Where do you come from?"

Disarmed, I replied, "New Mexico. Albuquerque."

"Sure. Al-bu-quer-que." He enunciated each syllable with care. Then he moved closer so that our knees touched. Still speaking slow Spanish, he introduced himself. "I am Hector, the stage manager. You're here for the show? Yes. Flamenco is life. Makes all the rest possible. Right? Every day, I watch a performance. It keeps me living. Otherwise, it all just sits in here." Hector placed his left hand over his heart. "Not good." He reached out and took my hand boldly. "So glad to meet you. Your name?"

"Stephany."

He released my hand and stood up, giving me a small but nevertheless theatrical bow. "Well, I must get to work. It's time."

He scurried off as a busload of noisy French tourists filed expectantly into the room. I hurried to finish what I had been writing in my journal. *There is a tribal feeling of belonging in this flamenco world. This is strange because flamenco people can be curt, impatient, and competitive. Yet always I feel the acknowledgment of a shared passion that unites us. We share a common ground.*

Soon every seat was filled, and Hector brought more folding chairs to accommodate the sudden overflow. Glad to be seated in the second row's center seat, I put away my notebook and waited with the now hushed and expectant audience. The troupe entered single file, two young male dancers, a guitarist, and a singer. They sat and found their centers, looking away from the staring audience. These first moments shifted the scattered energy in the room and quieted us.

The singer, a young man in his twenties with lustrous dark eyes and long curly hair, joined his hands together in front of his face. He turned his face slightly to the right before humming his first throaty but resonant note. The dancers shifted in their seats and sat taller, leaning slightly forward, as they began their *palmistas*. With the first notes of the guitar, I was swept away—we were all swept away—into the joy and beauty of flamenco.

A ripple of excitement, like wind across tall grasses, flowed through the audience. When the male dancer slowly rose, his arms ascending over his head, the women behind me gasped with awe, then called out bawdily, "*Olé, gitano!*" The boundary between audience and performer was eclipsed. The space of enchanted time, both sacred and libidinous, included everyone in moments of *duende* that illuminated and shone like stars in a moonless sky.

In an old section of Sevilla is a traditional flamenco bar. At midnight they say a group prayer, and then the dancing begins. This ceremony heightens the spirit of flamenco. All things must pass. Days end. The show begins in night's blackest, most tender heart. If I return to Sevilla, and I hope I do, I will find this *tablao*. I will stay up all night and walk back to my lodgings at dawn. I will participate in this midnight ceremony. In the meantime, it comforts me to know that somewhere in this world this ritual continues, lighting the way into darkness. This inspires me to continue to live with passion and imagination. I hope to stand tall and dance with life until that final date when the bull and I meet in the August sun and blood spills as it must into the eternal river of life.

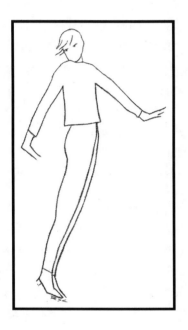

Chapter Twelve
The Promise

The mountain changes its moods: sometimes it is
dark and unfriendly, and sometimes it radiates
joy. But it is always alive, always alive.
—Mabel Dodge Luhan, *Lorenzo in Taos*

Ernesto Hernandez, or "Ernie," the principal dancer in the flamenco company at the Old Spaghetti Factory, looked down from the stage and smiled at me with his impish, gap-toothed grin. Ernesto was a sexy man, with a small waist and a perfectly proportioned body. He had a true Gypsy face—dark eyes, swarthy skin, and a mop of black hair. His sly, seductive smile is what I remember most. When he extended his hand, beckoning me to get up on the stage and dance with the troupe in their closing number, I shook my head and averted my gaze. The smoky darkness concealed my adolescent distress. The moment passed. Over the years I have returned to the memory with its poignant mixture of joy and regret.

At fourteen, intoxicated with music and dance, I was taking private flamenco lessons with Isa Mura, one of the dancers in the troupe. Whereas Ernesto was a comic, bawdy dancer, Isa was intense and deeply mystical. Isa had a strong, lean, angular body and face. She wore her long black hair pulled back in a bun, not a hair out of place. Maybe she put pomade on it to make it slick and shiny because it shone like a raven's wing. Her wide mouth, heavily painted with red lipstick, expressed neither happiness nor sadness but an inscrutable mixture of the two. When she smiled, though that was seldom, it was like seeing butterflies in sunlight. Her movements were sharp and clean, her almond-shaped, heavily made-up eyes aloof as a cat's.

Before the shows, she sequestered herself away in her bedroom in her small apartment a few blocks from the Flamenco de la Bodega. She had three young children, and they knew better than to interrupt her. No one disturbed her during those times. Her mother watched the children, visitors lowered their voices, and Isa would commune with the spirit that gave her the power to dance flamenco. I knew from watching Isa prepare and from watching her dance that flamenco was serious business. On the other hand, I knew from watching Ernesto's clowning on stage that flamenco had an irreverent, taunting quality. Irreverent, taunting, sexy, or serious, flamenco was passionate and emotional at a level I had never encountered before.

I longed to be part of the tight-knit flamenco world. After the show, the troupe would all hang out, usually at Richard Waylen's home and art studio, continuing to talk and make music until dawn. Jeff Chin, a young guitarist from the projects in the heart of Chinatown, would be folded over his guitar playing chords or would play intricate, classical pieces on his lute. Of course, at fourteen and then fifteen, I managed to stay out late only a few times. Yet I will never forget those nights of romantic promise.

Now, a half century later, when I take *cuadro* classes, I still feel shy when I am called out to perform in the circle. Being seen and expressing myself in front of an audience, no matter how small, still intimidates me. How could this be? I want to heal my long-standing inhibitions. Training and technique bring me to the possibility of dancing my own dance. It is remarkable how certain limitations persist.

Ernesto's invitation remains an open ticket. Something in my life still beckons. D. H. Lawrence often describes his characters' emotions through flower imagery. His people either bloom or wither, depending on their choices. Usually, the characters who resist change and repress their inner voices become stagnant and brittle, even violent. They enforce obsolete codes and eat too many chocolates or seek what Lawrence called "the bitch goddess" of fame and fortune. They judge and frown and dominate the cultural landscape. The characters who develop and break out of stagnant relationships and situations often experience hardship and uncertainty but always experience moments of *duende*, the harbinger of renewal.

Crisis and chaos often accompany these changes. Old structures need to be destroyed so that new things can be born and flourish. In Lawrence's novella *The Virgin and the Gypsy*, the river floods a village and forces everyone out of their houses in search of dry ground. The Victorian houses, with their heavy Victorian furniture and Persian carpets, are no match for the raw power of the floodwaters. Only the Gypsies, who are passing through in their colorfully painted wagons, are able to move easily to safety. And of course, a handsome Gypsy, seeing the maiden imprisoned in her family house, rescues her and then liberates her from her cumbersome virginity.

Each time I take a few steps inside the *cuadro* circle, each time I say yes to the invitation to dance, I experience the sensation of shedding a burden. People like Ernesto are teachers and guides who come and invite me to escape old inhibitions. These guides also appear in my dreams as different men. The psychologist Carl Jung might label them "animus figures." Some are kindly, gentle, subtle, and ever so attentive and wooing. Others are also tricksters who seduce and betray and even frighten me.

I read a newspaper story a few years ago about a Harvard doctor who died in Africa. The story goes something like this: A doctor who was married to an invalid for many years struggled with his wife's condition and eventually his own bouts of depression. When his wife died, he retired from his academic job and moved to Africa. Realizing a cherished dream, he set up a clinic for infectious diseases. He met a nurse, fell in love, and decided to marry. He and his new bride took a trip down the river with experienced native guides on their honeymoon. The guides watched carefully as their oars slid seamlessly through familiar waters, alert for the occasional hippo. Without warning, a huge alligator jumped up and snatched the doctor right out of the canoe. No one else was harmed. The guides had never seen such a thing, ever. The doctor was never seen again.

Now when my sister and I talk in code about someone's fortunate misfortunes or even our own, we say, "You don't escape the alligator." I have repeated the story on a variety of occasions, mostly to illustrate what the Buddhists refer to as impermanence. We never know how things will turn out or even how long we have to live. We can never out-guess fate. This truth, especially as I age, gives me courage to follow my heart's calling and let it take me where I need to be, even if that is an appointment with an alligator. I don't know why I say "even if." It is always an appointment with the alligator or the bull since death is inevitable.

What I find amazing about this story, in addition to the way the doctor died, is that he worked hard to get to that final meeting with his destiny. He died probably happier than he had been for many years, but he didn't escape the alligator. I venture to state that the lucky ones meet the alligator head on while gliding down a river, sitting beside their beloved. The lucky ones die in their suit of lights, the crowds cheering in the stands. They live richly until the very end.

I decide to go to another yoga and writing retreat in Taos. I am excited to see two friends from the previous year. These East Coast women, though older than I, live with admirable courage and a sense of adventure. We are going to share the "gate-keeper's cottage," a small house at the back of the main house. Equipped with a full kitchen, two fireplaces, and a living room, the cottage will provide a communal refuge for us in the evenings. We can gossip, drink wine, and relax together.

I am going to this retreat looking for a sign. My work on D. H. Lawrence has drawn me first to Taos and then to live in New Mexico. Living in New Mexico, I found flamenco. New questions are beginning to form. Something keeps drawing me back to the Mabel Dodge Luhan house, to my original interest in D. H. Lawrence. Taos both attracts and repels me. It seems to be a place of crossings and boundaries and invisible forces.

The preparation for the retreat has a ritual aspect. I gather my papers, my pens and ink, my dreams and intentions. The night before I leave, I have another of my lost dreams. I've been having them for a few months. No matter what is happening, I am not prepared. I have lost my ticket, haven't packed, have forgotten where I am going. These dreams make me wonder, *Where am I going? What do I need for a successful passage?* In this dream the night before my departure, I have forgotten my own address and think, *Next time you set off, just write it down on a slip of paper and put it in your pocket!*

I pick my friends up from their hotel, and we drive to Taos. As I listen to their conversation, I think about my reasons for this retreat. Outside of being with people I like, I want to get some muscle back into my creative habit, to return to the page and remember the writer in me. Doing yoga and writing seems to work. I know these five days spent working in a supportive and focused environment will recharge me and my creative life.

No experience is the same twice. Though I recognize familiar faces and enjoy the company of my friends, the focus of the retreat seems contrived, and I resist. Our teacher wants us to bond, to become a "wild pack." In a group of eleven women and one man (not counting our teacher), his encouragement seems slightly ridiculous. Doesn't he know that women do that without being told, that such bonding is instinctive and follows its own natural course?

I find myself avoiding group projects, seeking solitude, and wandering away from the pack.

The first morning after breakfast, I sit on a wooden bench in the middle of a patch of grass that has yet to recover from winter. I don't see a single pigeon in Mabel's pigeon coops. Magpies chatter, and an industrious woodpecker works the bark of an old cottonwood, still leafless. Everything is vigor and morning, cool and distinct, in the transition from winter to spring. Clouds confer with one another before taking off in their designated directions for the day. Two pigeons finally emerge from their homes and walk the roofline before flying off. Out come a few more, dancing their funny circle dances in front of their little round doorways.

During one of the afternoon times for writing, I find a quiet spot in the main house and a comfortable seat on Mabel's couch in her cozy, book-lined living room. I study the thick adobe walls with their photographs of Mabel and Tony. My gaze is drawn to a photograph of Tony. He is draped in a blanket from head to toe, only his handsome and serene face exposed. His presence is as visible as hers in this house, his image always next to hers, whether in a painting or in a photograph. I wonder why the focus is always on Mabel and why it is always called "Mabel's house." I sense his presence in this silent room, and with this comes a feeling of being admitted into the less visible realm of "Tony's house." I start to hear the older stories that flow below the surface, stories that connect this place to the land beneath it and the Taos Pueblo next door. Maybe the boundary is purely artificial and something drawn up by the whites' notion of ownership.

I browse a book on the coffee table whose cover bears a large photograph of Mabel and Tony. Unlike the photograph on the wall, taken when Tony was young and handsome, the cover photo shows him sitting on a rocking chair, an elderly and slightly overweight man wearing Western clothes and an enormous feather headdress. Mabel sits in a matching rocker, looking like an East Coast matron, her hair curled, her face soft with time. As I leaf through the pictures in the book, I see a photograph of a house that Mabel built on her property for D. H. Lawrence. It is called "the pink house" because of the color of the stucco. I knew about it but didn't realize that the house I'd been staring at from Mabel Dodge's house was *that* pink house.

I bring the book to the receptionist and ask her where this house might be. When she describes it, I realize I have seen it all along, but like Tony's portraits, for some reason I haven't fully noticed it. It has been just one more scrabbly adobe in a cluster along the west side of the road leading to the main house. And now it is so faded that it can hardly be called pink. The receptionist, a woman with great knowledge about the history of this place, asks if I would like her to call over to the artist who lives there. "He might let you walk around the property. It's best to call first."

When she calls him, she introduces me as a Lawrence expert and gets the green light for my excursion. I walk over and find a tall, spry man about my age waiting on his porch. He unexpectedly invites me in. For the next hour I get a tour of the house. There is a cupboard that Lawrence hand-painted with a phoenix. The fireplace in the studio, built by Tony and his friends from the pueblo, is an architectural wonder, designed so that no smoke ever backs into the house. I learn that many famous people have slept here over the years, including Carl Jung. My guide owns the house, but he has maintained the original character. He points out with pride the undulating bricks in the kitchen. The old cottonwoods around the house died off, and the roots under the kitchen withered, changing the surfaces of the floor.

When I leave, I walk over to the labyrinth. I enter asking a question: *Do I have permission to write about this place?* I look down and see a magpie feather at my feet. It is black and white and very incandescent in the sun. I pick it up. I will give it back to the center. As I reach the edge of the labyrinth, closest to the pueblo's edge, I find a magpie wing. It startles me. It almost shouts, "You are welcome, but this is no simple matter. This will teach you how to see two worlds and learn things usually out of reach of human consciousness. Are you really ready for this?" I look around, wondering if someone put this wing in my path to trick me. Two magpies in the cottonwoods above watch me, uncharacteristically silent.

I place the feather in the circle and cautiously walk past the wing on my way out of the labyrinth, as if I can ignore fate. I go back into Mabel and Tony's living room and begin to write. In her memoir *On the Edge of the Taos Desert*, Mabel tells the story of coming to Taos and meeting Tony. I find myself writing Tony's story, from his perspective.

On the night Tony foresaw Mabel's arrival, did he know he would be living in two worlds? I imagine him waking from the dream, leaving his sleeping family, and going outside to meet the sunrise. I can picture that Taos sky quivering with light and the mountain under a powder of fresh snow. How could he have known that he would love her, take care of her in her old age, one day marry her? His voice comes to me as if he has been waiting to tell his story.

> You ask me about that dream. I don't call them dreams. I do have spells, though, and I wander inside. My father was the same. I could travel with him sometimes when he left us, and I was the only one who could. It was nothing special because that is how I was born. I had no thoughts of traveling around from place to place all over the world the way these new people who come to Taos do. I don't even wonder too much about how they got so blown off course. They have been a problem sometimes, because they can be disrespectful and even dangerous. But those new ones, those artists, weren't like the rest. It made me want to shelter and protect them, the way I feel about wounded deer. Sometimes, though, I thought it would be best to kill them and put an end to their suffering. But I knew better than to have any part of it, or at least I thought I did until Mabel came to me.
>
> When I was a boy, I would stand beside the river. And the song in the river told me I would have to learn how to stay and leave at the same time. Sometimes I'd just pitch

rocks into the river, one after another until my arm went numb. It was all I could do to keep up with the force moving inside of me. Mabel always asked too many questions. When I told her the story of the way I threw rocks as a boy, she asked if I was nervous because I saw in my visions that people would come and change Taos. She asked if I wanted to stop them and felt frustrated because I knew I couldn't. She wasn't as bad as the rest of her friends, but she couldn't understand why her questions seemed stupid to me. She believed when I didn't answer that I was resigned or just not listening. She never understood that life wasn't up to me. It wasn't preordained either like some of her philosophy-minded friends seemed to think. My visions were more like Taos mountain. There is just no question or need for explanation.

I did have a few goals, though. I liked to figure out how to get the best deer meat or how to fish late into fall after other people gave up. It always pleased me to be "strategic" as Mabel called me. Sometimes when it went well like she wanted it to go, this word was a compliment. But when I disappointed her, or when as we got older, she started to walk away from me back to her own people and their ways, she believed I had tricked her into staying, into building our home, into giving her life to this place. I can't say it was a trick, but I did bring her here and share this place. The only trick was to let her think it was her idea.

As soon as Mabel arrived in that vision, I started to prepare. I had a notion I could expand my world to include her, the way I had learned to fish when everyone else gave up and went back home. I knew I'd stay with my family, my lands, my place. But I'd have to enlarge my patterns and weave her into my life. She had to be the visible one, the rich white woman who made things happen; otherwise, her people would stop us. Most people who come here leave. It never occurs to them they weren't invited to stay in the first place. They think they are leaving because their health fails, their marriage ends, or alcohol drives them crazy.

When I went inside and started the morning fire, I knew my family would have trouble understanding what I was about to do. I would be living with a white woman in the white world she would bring with her. I would still be home because, in truth, I never left. I would be adding on, increasing. Even Mabel never saw that. Only toward the end did she glimpse it. It made her mad. All along she had believed it was all her doing. I was sorry about that especially when her mind started to leave her and she didn't know who I was. We would be sitting together after dinner, and she would look over at me with a start. "Who is that Indian?" she would yell. "Get him out of here." I knew she didn't mean it. I would reassure whoever was there. I told them I took care of her. And I always did, until the end, until I knew I could begin my own path to the other world.

After that morning, I went about my life as I always did until the day I saw her standing in the yard. She was just moving into a house in town. I went home, got my drum, and set up outside her window. Mabel, in spite of all her money, was homeless. She sought a place to be. The fact that she had arrived with her husband, a weak man without much story in him, didn't matter. He was irrelevant. He knew it too, though he fussed when she left him. Sometimes if we quarreled, she said I drove him off and put a spell on her. But she saw me, too, in a dream before she came. She told me she knew I would be waiting here for her. I had the land all picked out. I visited it with my uncle many times as a boy. It was a special place, bordering as it did the far southern corner of the Pueblo. She bought it and we built her house here.

My family thought I married Mabel for her money. I had my Pueblo family, and Candelaria was a good wife and mother. Everything might have been all right if I hadn't married Mabel in a white man's way under their laws. It took me three years to decide it would keep us steady. Mabel needed that word for me, "husband." She needed me to be visible in her world, though I never was. Our marriage created quite a sensation in the news. One paper in the East did a big story about us that hurt Mabel but made me laugh: "Why Bohemian Queen Married Indian Chief." Mabel and her friends thought it was racist. I don't need to tell you what I thought.

I understood she needed her own house too. Women do. It had to be her place, bought with her money. She was a strong woman and, if you didn't oppose her, as generous as anyone I have ever known. Maybe that was because her people on the East Coast had all that money. Mabel never hoarded or kept tight accounts. She helped everyone she could help if they didn't get on the wrong side of her. She collected people, mostly writers and painters. Many of them had no place to go, their families broken and scattered. Few of them had money the way Mabel did. She liked having artists around her and wanted to help them stay. I never tried to stop her. The only time I openly opposed her was when D. H. Lawrence arrived. She tried her hardest to make him feel at home. I knew when I first saw him, his bones poking through his skin, that he was only going to be here a little time. And I saw right away he could never settle anywhere—a restless spirit. I respected him, though. He didn't pretend to be different with each person he met or try to get people to like him. He was a man I trusted. He didn't drink, didn't chase women or money. He wrote and talked ideas. Mabel liked both of those things.

The problem was I didn't like Mabel when she was around him. She got full of tangled thoughts and ideas, and her neurosis, as she called it, would come back. She saw a doctor in New York for this problem but was never completely cured. I couldn't be around her when she got like that, and I would leave. When she noticed my absence, she would realize she missed me and come find me. I had problems with Lawrence's wife Frieda too. She was a demanding woman. Lawrence's lungs were bad, and this made him peevish and mean. She kept drifting toward me. Mabel couldn't tolerate that. Frieda was jealous, too, but in a different way. Mabel wanted Lawrence's mind. We were not a comfortable foursome, right from the start. Frieda and Lawrence stayed in the house my brothers and I built for special guests. The women were too much alike to share the same yard. Finally, Mabel gave them a little ranch on some property to the north, and off they went. It wasn't hers to give, and she did it against my wishes. She could be that way sometimes.

They didn't stay there long either, though they claimed to be happy. It wasn't until Lawrence's death that Frieda came back with her Italian lover, Ravagli, and lived here until she died. Then her Italian returned to his wife and family in Italy a rich man. Lawrence's novels had started to sell. To keep Ravagli with her, Frieda left him half her estate. Mabel told me that the sexy book he wrote while he was dying made the most money of all. I never read the book, but knowing Lawrence, I'll bet he knew it would leave Frieda a rich woman and take her out of the poverty they had lived in all of their marriage. I liked him all the better for his generosity

beyond the grave and lack of jealousy. He
knew she would need to support her lover
if she wanted to keep him.

"Excuse me, am I disturbing you? Isn't this the most
lovely room?"

I come out of my reverie and look up. A gray-haired
woman with horn-rimmed glasses and a gray fur coat
stands in the doorway.

"No, not at all," I reply. Closing my notebook, I glance at
my watch. I am late again. Unbelievable since I am known
for my punctuality. I stand up, hugging my notebook to my
chest. Glancing at Tony's shrouded yet luminous photograph on the wall, I give silent thanks. I hurry to the dining
room, a big inviting space slightly lower than the rest of
the house. My friends have saved a chair for me at the end
of the long wooden dining room table. Their eyes register
relief when I walk in and sit down. I am suddenly glad I've
returned for another workshop even though it isn't going
the way I expected. The experience of *duende* in my writing
follows me like a presence into the spacious afternoon.

Chapter Thirteen
Shamans and Porcupines

To me life is a wild animal. You hope to
deal with it when it leaps at you.
—Keith Richards, *Life*

Some years ago, I took a vacation to Antigua, Guatemala, with the man I eventually would marry. I had spent several summers in Oaxaca, Mexico, during my marriage to my former husband years before. During those summers we often had contemplated taking the bus to Guatemala, but each time we had been told of the perils on the road. Bandits would stop the bus, make everyone get off, and then take their money and valuables. So when the opportunity arose to fly directly to Antigua under easier circumstances (I no longer was the mother of a young child), I knew I would be traveling to a dangerous place, even a decade later.

Because of my other times in Mexico and Latin America in the 1980s, I expected to see extreme poverty and men with guns. Even so, the men with semiautomatic rifles standing around in front of banks and shops in the older, tourist parts of the elegant colonial city subdued me. Our accommodations, though lovely, a hacienda style with a pool, had an armed guard at the entrance. The town itself, with its colorful colonial buildings and enormous carved wooden doors, invited cautious exploration. Stores large and small sold a variety of textiles in rich, exotic colors and designs, a feast for the eyes everywhere I looked.

My adventuresome boyfriend had not traveled in Latin America before. Always friendly and a bargain shopper, he struck up a conversation with a particular vendor standing outside one of the many tour/travel shops. He thought the price the young man quoted for a day trip that included a hike up a volcano was a great opportunity. The man, in his early twenties and dressed in jeans and a T-shirt that read "I Love New York," said in fluent English that he had gone to college to work in the tourism industry. Though I wanted him to succeed in his new career, I could not be persuaded. The State Department warned about the dangers lurking outside the city limits. Since I also had no interest in climbing active volcanos, I firmly but politely declined.

After ten days, I grew less vigilant. We had walked up and down the now familiar streets. We had found our favorite restaurants, including a wonderful café with a courtyard and fountain. A mural on one wall, in the bold style of Diego Rivera, depicted the history of Latin America before and after the Spanish Conquest, and I studied it as I ate my plate of fresh fruit and sipped my *café con crema*. I had shopped to my fill for handwoven and embroidered *huipils* made by the Mayan women in the mountain villages.

Once again, we sauntered back to our hotel after breakfast, past the friendly young vendor in another T-shirt that said "I Love LA." He made his usual pitch, including a new offer, two for the price of one. What a discount! Only for friends like us. He reassured us that there would be no more than six people in the van, including competent guides, and everything would be completely safe.

Why wouldn't I want to explore the countryside and see how the people lived, stop at a real Mayan village, climb an active volcano? Though I had no interest in the volcano part, I did want to see where these beautiful fabrics originated. Had I come all this way just to stroll the cobblestone streets of the city and sit in cafés? I am never quite sure what happens to me on these occasions, but there is a chink in my reason that propels me to say yes when I should say no. Even as I agreed, I believed I might still change my mind if and when I returned to my senses.

Back in our room, I glanced at the lush stack of intricately patterned *huipils*, all purchased over the last ten days. Each *huipil*, a simple traditional garment made and worn by the women, had a story—not only embroidered and woven into it but also in my memory of the purchase itself. On top was a white garment garlanded with blue birds and pink flowers, etched with golden threads. It glowed in light streaming through the small window that was set in the thick adobe wall. The maid had already come in, made the beds, swept the tile floors, and replaced the towels. I opened the little windows to air out the room, heavy with the pungent scent of Pine-Sol and lemon oil. Birds sang in the boughs of the magenta bougainvillea bushes cascading down the sides of the whitewashed building.

The previous evening, as we crossed a street for a better view of our favorite crumbling stone churches, a young girl with several folded garments in a wicker basket had smiled at us from the bottom steps. As soon as I smiled back, she was beside me, her basket a cornucopia of treasures at my feet. Out fluttered the most extraordinary, knee-length white *huipil* with silver and gold threads. As soon as I held it up to my face, an older girl who might have been her sister or even her mother appeared. She wore her hair coiled with colorful ribbons and braided on top of her head. She had the same sweetness of the younger girl, the same unbounded smile. We bartered, but not long, and soon the "best *huipil* yet" had been added to my collection.

The intricate, carefully crafted patterns on each *huipil* reflect hours, days, and perhaps months of patient, loving effort. Each holds a pattern that is both as rhythmic and as beautiful to behold as a poem or a prayer, a source of life. I wonder how much longer they will continue to weave the fabric on their portable backstrap looms and hand-embroider the patterns. Everything is changing, and more people must leave their villages in search of work in Guatemala City. Crowded into garbage-laden shantytowns, they struggle to survive. Handmade items may soon become collector's items. Indigenous peoples the world over are fast becoming indigent, displaced, and impoverished.

The night before our expedition to the volcano, I attended an art talk at one of the biggest textile stores in the city. A Mayan historian, a Guatemalan women in her thirties, explained the history and the meaning of the garments stacked five feet high around us and hanging from the walls. These fascinating rectangles of handmade cloth, folded and stitched at the sides, distinguished one community from the next. I learned the names of some of the patterns, all depicting elemental forces of nature. The Mayans, a shamanic culture like the aboriginal culture in Australia, heed their dreams. Supposedly, a woman at the beginning of the twentieth century was given the message in a dream to reintroduce this traditional garment and to teach other women the skills. She revived an ancient heritage that became a critical source of revenue for the women. My desire to learn more about the people who wove these textiles extinguished any lingering doubts I harbored about traveling into the countryside.

I dislike turning my life over to strangers. I like clean bathrooms, comfortable beds, and safe drinking water. I want to know that I can get off the bus, literally and figuratively, if the going gets rough. Certainly, we were both in pretty good shape. The worst that could happen, I reminded myself, was that we would be uncomfortable for a few hours. Or we might have to hand over our valuables to a desperately poor *campesino*, and we wouldn't be carrying much. Perhaps I had become overly cautious.

The next day, the guides picked us up a little before noon in a midsized van. It was a two-hour drive to the base of the volcano and a three-hour walk to the top, and they wanted us to get to the cone around sunset for the most dramatic effect. We would be walking back in the dark? As if reading my mind, the guide assured us that the trek was easy at night in the full moon's light.

The driver and his assistant sat in front. Three other people, two men and a woman, occupied the middle row, and we climbed into the back. *Well*, I thought, *one over the limit, not as bad as anticipated.* But we made another stop and then another. By the time we left the city, a crate had appeared so that yet another poor sucker could sit in the aisle next to the door. We rattled out of town, shoulder to shoulder, in the non-air-conditioned van in the heat of the afternoon.

We were the only Americans and the only people over fifty. One couple spoke in German, another in Russian, and the others spoke Spanish. The driver and his assistant joked together as we began our ascent through the dense jungle, bumping up a poorly paved, one-lane road. We passed several barefoot, furtive-looking *campesinos* carrying large bundles of wood on their backs. In their dark, unsmiling expressions, I saw myself as a rich, white foreigner stupid enough to vacation in such a starkly impoverished region. The gulf between our worlds opened up like a dangerous chasm, one I knew I could never bridge, especially as the thrill-seeking tourist I seemed to have become.

As if smelling our fear, the driver hit his companion on the shoulder with boyish familiarity. The next thing I knew, his companion was waving a semiautomatic rifle above his head and laughing. "See?" our driver announced gaily. "Nothing to worry about."

Of course, my stomach lurched, and I knew that we would be lucky to make it back alive. We had passed an invisible boundary into another world, where our ideas of law and order meant nothing. This feeling of no return reminded me of another time and place. I had flown to Punta Arenas, a Chilean city near the southern tip of South America. As the plane landed on the runway, we had looked out at the dark, cold, bleak landscape. All of the passengers seemed to sink down inside themselves. The reality of being in such an end-of-the-world place, a place that we had only barely imagined and so close to the South Pole, subdued us all. In a way, traveling to such places must be like going to the moon, a place of myths and dreams. A border is crossed between imagination and reality, and what awaits is strange and slightly menacing. Perhaps some territories are better left unexplored, fit for nursery rhymes and bedtime stories. But then again, such experiences bring with them a treasure trove of memories to be culled over a lifetime.

My boyfriend nudged me and brought me back to the present. "Look at that. He must be carrying twice his weight." He pointed out the window. An old man walked barefoot up the narrow winding road, a large bundle of branches on his back. He didn't glance in our direction as we passed. We had entered what I imagined to be Conrad's *Heart of Darkness*. Our companions, who had recently been engaged in lively conversations, grew silent and introspective.

We drove into a small village and parked near a crumbling church. On the slab stone steps to the entrance, an old woman wearing a red *huipil* over a long black skirt tended a smoldering fire. Her graying hair was braided and coiled across her head. Large plastic buckets filled with orange gladiolas lined the step behind her. Our guide told us that the fire was never allowed to go out. Though the church originally had been built and run by Catholics, the Mayans used it for their ceremonies and rituals.

Inside the church, the main altar had been removed.

Various rituals were in process, including some sort of dousing of a chicken in a crudely drawn circle on the floor. Incense burned, and candles flared. We had stepped into a different architecture of time and space, what Buddhists often refer to as groundlessness. With my familiar ways of organizing and understanding what I was seeing suspended, I watched and listened like a child.

At three in the afternoon, we arrived at the base of the volcano. We must have been higher than the five thousand feet of Antigua already, and now we would climb higher yet. I felt queasy and breathless as I stepped out of the van and looked up at the black mountain toward the flattened cinder-cone top. The mountain, devoid of all vegetation, was made entirely of volcanic rock and ash. I adjusted the straps of my backpack, hoping no one would notice the first of many tears that would slide down my cheeks that day. The driver and his assistant greeted a *campesino* with warm familiarity. The man rose from his resting place beneath the shade of a lone pine tree. He wore a white buttonless shirt, loose cotton pants, and handmade sandals. Though he was about my height and age, he was lithe and compact like a runner.

Our driver explained that Antonio lived in a village up the road and that he knew the volcano well. He would bring up the rear and make sure everyone stayed together. Our guides would lead. Antonio smiled at me, and his face lit up. I have rarely seen such radiance and peace in a face. He was coming with us. My panic subsided. I stopped worrying about being left behind. I stopped worrying about anything.

Without further instruction, we started up the slippery slope of the black mountain. The youngest, the two men and the woman from Spain, kept up with the steady pace of the guides. The Dutch couples followed a little behind. I struggled to keep up with the German man, who was not much younger than we were. He soon slowed his pace, reluctantly. It was a steep incline, and the air grew increasingly thin. When the German man stopped for a moment to pant, I tried to make a joke about our age, but he glared at me and returned to his determined adventure. I glanced back at my boyfriend, who plodded along with his head down, last in line. Antonio grinned and shrugged his shoulders as if to say, *This is the way this part of the story goes.*

Like walking at the beach on sand, my feet sank down with each step I took. Sharp, needlelike pain in my knees cautioned me. I had done enough climbing to know that the best method was to not look up at how far I still had to go. I tried to stay with my breath. If I pushed too hard too fast, I knew I wouldn't make it to the top. We were about an hour into the walk, and people were beginning to tire. My boyfriend, slightly overweight, found breathing difficult. When we took a short break, he informed the group that he couldn't continue and would wait for us to return from the top.

I didn't want to leave him, but he didn't want me to give up on continuing with the group. He assured us he would be fine, and gradually, we began our trek up the mountain without him. Now I was the last in line, Antonio following behind. We struck up a halting conversation since my Spanish was very limited. He explained to me that if we saw a porcupine on the trail, my boyfriend would find the energy to continue. I wasn't sure I had heard him right. A porcupine here?

As we circumvented a large boulder, Antonio explained that it had fallen just the week before when the volcano erupted. Erupted! A week ago! Yes, he said with a laugh, as though telling a good story. He also explained that the continuous eruptions had wiped out his village once, forcing them to relocate to another place nearby. When I asked why they still lived at the base of the volcano, he shrugged and replied that this was where they had always lived. Where else would they go? I had no answer for that, but I hoped the volcano wouldn't spit any stray boulders today.

The climbers at the front of the line stopped. When we caught up with them, they stood in a semicircle around a feisty, fat porcupine who lumbered at their feet. "Here he is," my guide said in Spanish in an affectionate tone.

I couldn't believe it. Where had this prickly creature come from? Where did he live? Maybe the guides fed him, and he knew when to show up. My boyfriend appeared, apparently completely revived. When he reached us, he said he had been resting when suddenly his strength returned. He knew he could make it to the top. The group passed around a few snacks, drank some water, and began the last half of the trek in the fading daylight.

My boyfriend walked in front of me, and Antonio walked at my side. Sometimes if I engage in a good conversation, I don't notice how difficult things actually are. Antonio must have sensed this, because he kept me talking, though both of us had some trouble with my level of Spanish. A single phrase or a word was all we needed to stay connected. As it grew darker, the smell of sulfur intensified, and with it came a vague nausea in the pit of my stomach. An overwhelming vulnerability descended on me. A shift started to happen in my perception. I am not kidding you—it seemed like Antonio became more and more like a father to me as I grew younger and younger.

Though I had never known my father, I had the uncanny experience of knowing my father. As this transformation was occurring, part of me noted that I was in an altered state. Yet the feelings that arose were fresh and true. I couldn't deny their emotional authenticity. Antonio was the father I had missed. How I had missed him too. How had I made it through my childhood without someone to sooth my fears and protect me from the great unknown? How could this humble man create such a feeling of familiarity and security for me?

I became acutely aware of the things I had missed growing up without a father. I had experienced this loss at such a young age that I hadn't even known what I had missed until now. Tears streamed down my face as I struggled up the unrelenting incline and as night descended, the heat disappeared, and the moon rose. How big the world had always felt, how unruly the demons, how afraid I had always been—so alone with my fears. What might it have been like to know the comfort of a father who could calm my fears with a good story and walk beside me no matter what?

That last hour hiking up the volcano with Antonio

taught me what it would have been like, and I realized the father I needed and wanted was a kind and gentle man, a steady man who knew how to live in the face of uncertainty. Guide, teacher, and father, Antonio's spirit sheltered and soothed me and helped me make it to the top. I didn't climb that mountain just to look into the hot mouth of the cone, though I did look. We had only our extra clothing across our mouths and noses to shield us from the toxic fumes, and people who stayed too long, staring down into that deadly cauldron, could get sick to their stomachs and faint.

I moved off with Antonio to a level spot and with his encouragement sat down and then stretched out on my back. My boyfriend sat a few yards away, his back against a rock. Others had drifted off into their own places and own worlds. Night at ten thousand feet surely must have been cold, but all I remember is Antonio standing quietly in the distance and the feeling of leaving my body as I floated into the brilliant, starry night sky with its radiant full moon. No more fear, no more self. I was gone. An incredible sense of well-being swept through me. Somewhere beyond words and time was the sense that such freedom and release might come again at my actual death.

Our guides signaled for us to descend. We gathered our belongings and filed down the slippery mountain. The only sounds came from the shifting black rock beneath our feet. Feeling that we were being followed, I glanced back and saw two men carrying machine guns pointed slightly toward us. Fear rippled through our group. Our guides informed us that these men were here to guard us going down since we were easy targets in the dark. Targets in the dark?

Antonio and I glanced at each other and shrugged. I accepted this as if we had just been told it was eight o'clock and forty degrees. Tears of sheer exhaustion streamed down my face, but I felt detached even from this. I just cried and cried, silently and profusely, as if a river was flooding its banks. It wasn't that I trusted life and had shed my deepest fears, but I felt safe enough to accept my utter powerlessness. What good would it do me to obsess over the fact I never should have come, that I should have known better? Old, entrenched coping mechanisms had vanished.

Our driver was already waiting inside the van at the base of the volcano. Everyone accounted for, we drove down the road to Antonio's village for a Coke or a beer before the drive back to Antigua. Antonio was just a regular man again, a tired *campesino* with a weathered face and downcast eyes. I knew from our journey up that he had already trekked up the mountain with a group earlier in the day. He was ready to go home. I no longer held onto him emotionally the way a little girl would to a parent. I was aware again of the others and the growing hunger in my belly—and of course, the need to use a restroom. Every joint and muscle in my body ached. I squeezed my boyfriend's hand, and he smiled, his eyes filled with love and recognition.

We stopped at a small, makeshift café in Antonio's village. A single lightbulb hanging from a wire illuminated the tiny patio area. I bought Antonio a Coke, and we said goodbye. Soon we had piled into the van, somewhat revived by the sugar or alcohol. People chatted quietly as we sped toward Antigua. It was too late for dinner when we got back to our hotel. So we walked down the street to a little local café and had tortilla soup and a beer. I don't remember tasting anything as delicious as that hot, spicy soup or anything more refreshing than that Corona beer in a frosted glass. My mind was still. I was incapable of making a single plan, directing a single drama. For that space in time, I was utterly at peace. I felt free and unencumbered in a way that I had never felt before. I had been into the heart of darkness and found my way home.

It is another summer in Albuquerque. It is hot, really hot. Hot and very dry. Now we also endure the smoke from forest fires to the north and the south. Global warming more than likely will make the Southwest a place to visit but not live. I've been considering living somewhere else, where water is abundant and the heat less merciless. Transitions are never easy for me. Maybe that is an understatement. Many days, weather alerts caution people to stay inside. What about the animals, the plants? The homeless?

I park my car and glance at the temperature reading on the top of the bank. It's 99 degrees at 5:50 p.m.! I grab my bag and check to make sure I brought my water bottle. I walk into the studio. The flamenco studio is not air-conditioned, relying on ceiling and floor fans to move the hot air across our sweating bodies. A dress rehearsal is in progress, and the singer and guitar player fill the space with powerful sound. Five of the principal dancers in the company are in the middle of a dance. One of my favorite teachers and dancers glides across the floor like a flame. Transported, I sit with a few other classmates at the edge of the stage and watch. We could be anywhere, a cave in Spain, a concert hall, a bodega in San Francisco in the 1960s.

The singer is a big man with a big spirit. Seeing he has an audience, he smiles and gives even more heart to his song. The guitar player shoots me a look of recognition, and I feel the circle draw around me, including me. I have forgotten this, these moments of shared understanding and passion. I know these people. We have danced together, and I have studied with them. Magic finds me in this hot, dusty studio. There is no place on earth I would rather be. More students straggle in and join our little audience. The dance ends, and we clap and clap with wholehearted enthusiasm. The troupe clears out so that the classes can begin.

I don't know how much longer I'll be living in this place, dancing with these people. I can see a time when this pattern will change, but not yet. I file down the narrow hall to the back studio. I sense a presence close behind me and turn slightly to see who it is. The singer grabs my shoulder and lets out a shout, giving me a start.

"You scared me to death," I say.

Undaunted, he replies, "No, I scare you to life!"

We laugh, both knowing he is right.

Bibliography

Baca, Jimmy Santiago. *A Place to Stand.* New York: Grove Press, 2001.

Butterfly, Julia. *The Legacy of Luna: The Story of a Tree, a Woman and the Struggle to Save the Redwoods.* New York: Harper Collins, 2001.

Bynner, Witter, trans. *The Way of Life According to Lao Tzu.* New York: Berkeley Publishing Group, 1994.

Collins, Larry, and Dominique Lapierre. *Or I'll Dress You in Mourning: The Story of El Cordobes and the New Spain He Stands For.* New York: Simon and Schuster, 1968.

Dodge, Mabel. *Edge of the Taos Desert: An Escape to Reality.* New York: Harcourt, Brace, 1937.

———. *Lorenzo in Taos.* Santa Fe: Sunstone Press, 2007.

Francis, John. *Planet Walker.* Washington, DC: National Geographic Society, 2005.

Garcia Lorca, Federico. "Play and Theory of Duende." In *Deep Song and Other Prose*, edited and translated by Christopher Mauer. New York: New Directions, 1980.

Harden, M. J. *Voices of Wisdom: Hawaiian Elders Speak.* Hawaii: Aka Press, 1999.

Heilbrun, Carolyn. *The Last Gift of Time: Life Beyond Sixty.* New York: Random House, 1997.

———. *Writing a Woman's Life.* New York: Random House, 1988.

Hillman, James. *The Soul's Code: In Search of Character and Calling.* New York: Random House, 1996.

Hirsch, Edward. *The Demon and the Angel: Searching for the Source of Artistic Inspiration.* New York: Harcourt, 2002.

Jordan, Mary, and Kevin Sullivan. *The Prison Angel: Mother Antonia's Journey from Beverly Hills to a Life of Service in a Mexican Jail.* New York: Penguin, 2005.

Lawrence, D. H. *Lady Chatterley's Lover.* New York: Bantam Books, 1968. Originally published in Florence, Italy, 1928. Banned in the Unites States until 1959 and in England until 1960.

———. *Women in Love*. New York: Dover, 2002. Originally published in London by Secker Ltd.

Le Clair, Anne D. *Listening to Noise: The Transformative Power of Silence*. New York: Harper Collins, 2009.

Morca, Teodoro. *Becoming the Dance: Flamenco Spirit*. Costa Rica: Teodoro Morca, 2004.

Richards, Keith. *Life*. New York: Little, Brown, 2012.

Sackville-West, Vita. *All Passions Spent*. New York: Virago Press, 1983.

Tharp, Twyla. *The Creative Habit: Learn It and Use It for Life*. New York: Simon and Schuster, 2003.

Weber, Jason. *Duende: A Journey into the Heart of Flamenco*. New York: Broadway Books, 2003.

Woolf, Virginia. *A Room of One's Own*. New York: Harcourt, 1929.

Printed in the United States
By Bookmasters